THE BLUESMEN

ALSO BY SAMUEL CHARTERS

Jazz: New Orleans

The Country Blues

Jazz: The New York Scene

The Poetry Of The Blues

Poetry

The Children

The Landscape At Bolinas

Days As Thoughts In A Season's Uncertainties

The Bluesmen
by Samuel Charters

The story and the music
of the men who made the Blues

OAK PUBLICATIONS, NEW YORK

Book design by Jean Hammons

Photographs on pages 24, 146 and 164 by Ann Charters

1st PRINTING

© 1967 Oak Publications
701 Seventh Ave., New York, N. Y. 10036

Library of Congress Card Catalogue Number: 67-24017

Printed in the United States of America for the Publisher by Faculty Press, Inc., Brooklyn, N. Y.

FOR PETE WHALEN

I ... was obliged to sit all day without victuals in the shade of a tree; and the night threatened to be very uncomfortable, for the wind rose and there was great appearance of heavy rain, and the wild beasts are so very numerous in the neighborhood, that I should have been under the necessity of climbing up the tree and resting among the branches. About sunset, however, as I was preparing to pass the night in this manner, and had turned my horse loose that he might graze at liberty, a woman, returning from the labours of the field, stopped to observe me; and perceiving that I was weary and dejected, inquired into my situation, which I briefly explained to her; whereupon, with looks of great compassion, she took up my saddle and bridle and told me to follow her. Having conducted me into her hut, she lighted up a lamp, spread a mat on the floor, and told me I might remain there for the night. Finding that I was very hungry she said she would procure me something to eat. She accordingly went out and returned in a short time with a very fine fish; which having caused to be half broiled upon some embers, she gave me for supper. The rites of hospitality being thus performed towards a stranger in distress, my worthy benefactress (pointing to the mat, and telling me I might sleep there without apprehension) called to the female part of her family, who had stood gazing on me all the while in fixed astonishment, to resume their task of spinning cotton; in which they continued to employ themselves a great part of the night. They lightened their labour by songs, one of which was composed extempore; for I was myself the subject of it. It was sung by one of the young women, the rest joining in a sort of chorus. The air was sweet and plaintive, and the words, literally translated, were these: "The winds roared, and the rain fell. The poor white man, faint and weary, came and sat under our tree. He has no mother to bring him milk; no wife to grind his corn. Chorus - Let us pity the white man; no mother has he." Etc. Etc...

Mungo Park
"Travels In The Interior Districts of Africa" 1799

People keep asking me where the blues started and all I can say is that when I was a boy we always was singing in the fields. Not real singing, you know, just hollerin', but we made up our songs about things that was happening to us at that time, and I think that's where the blues started ...

Son House, 1965

Contents

Introduction

When I began this study more than two years ago my intention was to revise and expand my earlier book "The Country Blues;" since in the five years that had passed since it was published a considerable amount of new material on the blues and the blues singers had been discovered by dozens of researchers working both in the South and in the northern city slums where many of the singers now are living. It was not until I began the actual writing of the book that I realized how much material had been gathered. There were articles in music magazines, in teen-age fan magazines, in jazz magazines, in local coffee house schedules, in folk festival programs, and there was even more material in the liner notes for the hundreds of blues and folk albums that have been released over the last few years. It has been one of the most extensive, the most fruitful, and the most exciting research programs ever done in the field of folk music, and it has come - for once - in time to get answers to some of the most difficult problems in the development and the growth of the blues idiom. It was too late to do much more than trace the earliest sources and forms of the blues, but it was possible to learn some of the patterns of change and emphasis as the blues has moved - in less than sixty years - from rough field singing to the contemporary Chicago blues band style.

It is particularly interesting that all of this research has been done by people whose only real interest was in the blues. Most of them are still in their twenties, many of them are blues musicians, and usually they've had to do their research on a well-frayed shoestring. The universities and the foundations have not contributed anything to the work that has been done, and have generally even tried to discourage students who wanted to do independent research in the field. The blues is still too strong and too vital an expression for the university world to feel comfortable with it. Nearly all of the important recording that was done of blues singers in the 'twenties and the 'thirties was done by the commercial record companies, and it has been to a great extent the recording activities of a few independent companies that have helped contribute to the field trips and the documentation that has been done in recent years. Moses Asch, at Folkways, has, of course, continued to make it possible to record the older singers and to do extensive interviews with them, and Robert Weinstock, at Prestige Records, devoted a "Blues-ville" series to recordings of both older blues men and younger men still singing in the older styles. The folklorist Kenneth Goldstein, who was in charge of the series, sent researchers to nearly all of the major blues areas and gave them a free hand in working with the singers and their music. The result was not often a successful commercial recording, but the amount of information that was gathered more than justified the effort. Also the individual collectors working to gather material for their own small record companies - Chris Strachwitz of Arhoolie Records, Bob Koester of Delmark Records, Harry Oster of Folk-Lyric, Dick and Louisa Spottswood of Piedmont, Pete Welding of Testament, John Fahey and Ed Denson of Takoma - have all made important contributions to the growing body of knowledge about the blues.

I have tried to acknowledge some of the help I've gotten from the writing and the interviewing of these determined and sometimes indefatigable researchers in "The Blues Men" itself, but I would also like to acknowledge their assistance here. Among the people who have been of considerable help to me with advice and assistance of every kind have been Pete Whalen, Bill Givens, George Mitchell, Stefan Grossman, Don Kent, Bob Koester, Pete Welding, Dick and Louisa Spottswood, Nick Perls, Dick Waterman, Charles O'Brien, and Charlie Musselwhite. Through their articles or field collecting I have also been greatly helped by Arthur Rosenbaum, Gayle Dean Wardlow, Chris Strachwitz, Lawrence Cohn, David Mangurian, Julius Lester, John Fahey, Ed Denson, and Barry Hansen.

Also it would have been considerably more difficult to discuss the blues recordings themselves without the important work that was done in England by Robert M. W. Dixon and John Godrich, in assembling their detailed and exhaustive discography of blues and gospel recordings to 1942. The book, "Blues & Gospel Records, 1902 - 1942," published by Brian Rust in 1963, is an indispensible research tool for anyone working in the blues field, and all record data in this study has been checked against their listing. The work of Pete Whalen and Bill Givens, with their series of reissues on the Origin Jazz Library label, has also been of great importance in making available for study some of the greatest - as well as the rarest - of the early blues recordings.

The amount of material that all of these researchers have found is so extensive that I have had to divide this study of the male blues singers into three volumes. This first volume discusses the singers and the styles from Mississippi, Alabama, and Texas up to the second World War, with a brief consideration of some of the traceable relationships between the blues and African song. Volume Two will be concerned with:

1. The Atlantic Coast - Georgia and the Carolinas.
2. Memphis and the Tennessee singers.
3. St. Louis and Arkansas.
4. The development of the urban blues in Chicago before 1942.

11

The third volume will end the study with:

1. The post war blues in Chicago and Detroit.
2. The growth of the California and Texas post war styles.
3. The women singers in the country style.
4. The folk blues artists, among them John Hurt, Leadbelly, and singers found in recent years by field collectors.

When the broad outlines of the growth and the development of the blues have finally been sketched in it will be possible to look more intensively at some of the aspects of the blues - musical, textual, and sociological - which have given the music its strength and its emotional expressiveness; so the work of the last volumes is being pushed to completion. The people working in the blues field sometimes seem to pile up new material even faster than it can be read, but in the growing literature of the blues the outlines of stylistic growth emerge more and more clearly, despite the long years that have passed since the blues was still a young, half-formed song style.

Samuel Charters
June, 1966
New York, N.Y.

12

A Note on the Musical Examples

As the blues is essentially an Afro-American musical idiom it is very difficult to transcribe the music into the standard Euro-American system of scales, rhythms, and note values. These transcriptions have tried to keep as close as possible to the original, although the singer may be singing in a concert pitch that has little relationship to the guitar key that he is playing in; since the guitar is tuned to itself, and not to a fixed pitch instrument. In many of the pieces a tone of the scale is a "neutral tone," neither major nor minor, as in the various European scales. These tones have been marked with an (x) above the staff, and the best way to approximate their sound is to strike both the major and the minor of the note on a piano simultaneously and listen to the resulting mixed tone.

Since the blues is strongly colored with the harmonic patterns of the work songs and the hollers from which it developed, the harmonic structure of the purest country blues can only occasionally be approximated by conventional chord symbols. Usually the guitar is in a local tuning, and often the finger picking syle makes any kind of elaborate harmonic movement extremely difficult. For many of the blues there is no change in the accompaniment harmonies and the only chord change is suggested in the voice. Because of this nearly all of the examples have been left without chord symbols. It would be misleading to suggest that these pieces can be played with conventional guitar harmonies, and the sound would be uncomfortably distant from the complex structure of the original performance. The country blues is a highly individual style, rather than communal folk music. For someone who is interested in the accompaniments, the recordings themselves, along with the descriptions of the tunings and the styles with the individual examples, will be the most helpful.

13

A Note on the Musical Examples.

THE AFRICAN BACKGROUND

One of the most distinctive song forms that has grown out of the confusion and the violence of the twentieth century is the blues of the American Negro. The blues is not only a musical expression, but as a unique song style it is also a social expression; since the existence of a separate body of Negro song within the larger American culture is an insistent reminder of the separateness of the Negro himself in American society. Since he has been forced to live outside of the majority culture he has developed his own culture, and found within the difficulties and the pain of his experience the materials for a rich and vital music. Of all the forms of contemporary Negro music in the United States it is the blues which is still most closely related to the noisy emotional directness of everyday life, and it is also the musical form most closely related to the African song styles which were its most immediate cultural heritage, despite other influences on its development.

On a Friday afternoon, November 26, 1936, in San Antonio, Texas, a young Negro singer still in his teens, named Robert Johnson, recorded a song that he called "Cross Road Blues." "I went to the crossroads, fell down on my knees ... I asked the Lord above, have mercy, save poor Bob if you please." He was accompanying himself with a guitar, playing it with a metal slide on the little finger of his left hand in the Mississippi "bottleneck" style. His vocal style and the melodic line of the verse were African in the hard, intense tone and the descending pattern of the phrase. The melodic scale, a gapped hexatonic scale pattern, was African. At the beginning of the second line of the third verse, "Uumh, oh dark gone catch me here," he used a nasal falsetto tone that was probably derived from even earlier Islamic influences on African music. The guitar itself was European, but the rhythmic style and the tuning, an open, almost lyre-like tuning, used both African and European elements. The complex interrhythmic relationships in the accompaniment were related to the complex drumming patterns of much African music, but the strong emphasis on the four-beat measure

15

unit and the harmonic structure was European. The use of an open tuning
was similar to the tunings of the West African harps and lyres and small
metal keyed thumb "pianos," but in his tuning the strings outlined a
European harmonic triad. His use of a bottleneck to play a melodic line
in unison with the voice could have been influenced by the high, whining
one-string Arabic instruments that were used to accompany singing
along the slave coast, or by the country fiddle styles of the American
South, which also repeated the melody behind the vocal line. The verse
form of the blues used the English elements of a loose pentameter rhythm
and terminal rhyme, but the pattern of two repeated lines and a final
rhyming line was unique to the blues. The language was an American
regional dialect, and the emotional situation that produced his song was
the law in Mississippi that forced all Negroes off the roads at sundown.
Even in its isolation within the Negro community the blues is a vivid
example of the many-leveled acculturation that has characterized
the growth of American society.

The African presence in the blues can only be distantly glimpsed, like
the sun as it drifts through the clouds on a hazy morning. Nearly two
centuries have passed since there was extensive movement from Africa
to the then new United States, and in this long period of tumult and up-
heaval the music of Africa, as well as the music of the African in
America, has changed. How much, and in what ways, will always be
difficult to tell. There was no careful field documentation of either
musical style until well into the Twentieth Century. Between African
ritual singing, however, and a blues club like Pepper's Lounge in Chicago's southside Negro slum, there was a long and complex development of
music within the slave culture, and elements of this older music still
could be found among southern work gangs, often in prisons, when the
first efforts at documentary recording were done in the late 'twenties.
The pattern of development was clearly from the African communal
song to the slave work song, and from the work song to the blues. It is
also now becoming evident, as the first extensive work is being done in
African music, that there was a widespread solo song style in West
Africa that was probably the strongest influence on the solo blues
style that emerged from the work song. Often these were "praise
songs," that described an important man's fields and houses and cattle,
and the singers sometimes had a professional status in the community.
"... The Manding people for one, have had praise-singers for centuries.
These singers either attach themselves to particular men of influence,
such as powerful Moslem marabouts (religious leaders) and wealthy
merchants, or travel independently from town to town singing at
marriages and other fetes. Those who travel spread news, gossip, and
sing the praise of their patron throughout a wide area. Singing with the
accompaniment of a twenty-stringed instrument called a kora, they perform compositions of their own, making up the words as they go along.
They extemporize with ease, using a huge wealth of stock phrases and
metaphors that are combined and recombined in an infinite number of
ways."[1]

Among the Ila and the Tonga people, the solo song forms were even more closely related to the blues that were to develop on another continent more than a century later, not only musically, but also as a concept of an individual song style developing in the midst of a communal music tradition. Both the men and the women had personal songs that they performed at the "beer drink" parties. The woman's song form, the Impango, was high and fast, the men's, the Ziyabilo, was sung very slowly, usually unaccompanied, but sometimes the man singing would play a small drum. The women's songs were more directly involved with the social occasion. A woman would decide that she wanted to have an Impango to sing about her husband, usually praising him for his strength and his possessions. When she had decided on the things that she wanted in the song she and her friends went to someone in the village who was regarded as skillful in making songs and told the other person - usually a woman - what she wanted in her piece. The other woman would accept a gift and tell her to return in two or three weeks. When the woman came back she brought her friends with her again and the woman who had made the Impango would begin to teach it to her, line by line. Usually it took several sessions before the woman had her song memorized, and she brought her friends with her so that they could learn it as well and prompt her if she forgot some of it. Then, when she'd learned it, she practiced it to herself until she was ready to perform it. When a new song was performed at a beer drink there was considerable excitement and friends and relatives either interrupted her to give her presents, or-if they were too poor to give anything - to sing their own Impango as a compliment to her. This wide spread style of singing was one of the few areas of solo performance within a communal framework in West Africa.

The men's songs, the Ziyabilo, were more diverse in subject than the women's songs. Often the men made up songs as they spent hours alone tending cattle or mending fishnets. The songs were "... a meandering sort of tune in a free rhythm," a phrase which could almost be a description of the American field "holler," a slow, introspective song form of the slave period that survived in the southern prisons. The men alone in the fields with the mules, or breaking up the dirt between the cotton rows, sang to themselves in loosely rhymed verses that had a "meandering" feel to their drifting, irregular rhythms.

As early as 1915, John Work, in his "Folk Song Of The American Negro," [2.] had noticed the relationships between the melodic scales used in African and Afro-American music. In a chopping song of the Kroo people, sung by three or four men as they stood around a tree with their axes, (the same way that the chopping was done on the slave plantations), he found that the scale used only five notes, omitting the fourth and the seventh tones of the European seven-note diatonic scale and altering the third tone to a sound that was somewhere between the European major and minor modalities. These "gapped pentatonic" scales were as widely used in the South as they were in Africa. Work even went so far as to say that the scale used in Afro-American music was only the African scale with a flatted seventh tone used harmonically. The scale patterns in the South, however, were considerably more varied, and reflected the diverse African cultures that had been engulfed by the slavers. A group of work songs collected in the Carolinas in the 1920's showed some of the range of the folk scales. [3.]

Example 1.

Lower auxiliary

The blues, as a melodic form, has tended to group around the pentatonic scales, and this same pentatonism has been noted in other areas where there is a strong body of African influenced music. An ethnomusicologist in Venezuela has written of the Negro music of the Venezuelan coastal areas: "... The melodies of these songs, so far as they have been studied, present certain universal characteristics, such as pentatonism and melodic independence." [4.] African music, probably because of its strong outside influences, is no longer as dominated by five and six-note scales as it seems to have been in an earlier period of development. In 1958, however, Hugh Tracey, in an analysis of the scales used by eighty African tribes, found that thirty-three of the tribes still used pentatonic scales for their entire musical expression, and that although the other tribes studied also used six and even seven-note scales, there was still a widespread use of the five-note scales for much of the vocal music. [5.]

The melodic outline of the blues also seems to have a base in the African singing styles. A.M. Jones, in his description of African melody, could also have been describing a general characteristic of the blues.

> *Broadly speaking, the outline of an African tune is like a succession of the teeth of a rip-saw; a steep rise (not usually exceeding a fifth) followed by a gentle sloping down of the tune; then another sudden rise - then a gentle sloping down, and so on. The tendency is for the tune to start high and gradually to work downwards in this saw-like manner.* [6.]

In an analysis of two hundred and fifty-nine blues melodies it was found that nearly two hundred of them had the same pattern of descending from a higher melodic tone that Jones had noticed in Africa. Of the two hundred and fifty-nine melodies studied, one hundred and ninety-one were in this category, twenty used a compound verse that delayed the introduction of the usual descending line with two lines of half-spoken recitative, eight used the same fast country dance melody, and the last twelve used a variety of other melodies. There may be some relationship between this melodic approach and the African method of singing scales from the highest to the lowest notes, rather than in ascending patterns as in the European practice. This descending line was common in African music, in the American work song, in the Venezuelan Negro song, and in the blues.

Example 2.

There was also in Africa a strong tradition of guitar-like instruments, and most of the early accompaniment styles in the blues seem to have grown from the rhythmic finger picking styles that had been developed in West Africa. The instrument was introduced into Africa by the Portuguese in the fifteenth or sixteenth century in its earliest European form as the small "machet" or rabequina. Using this as a model the African musicians built crude guitars that were called rabekin, ramakienjo, raamakie, rampi, rabouquin, or ramki. The first traveler's mention of the instrument was in 1733, but it had clearly been played along the coast for many years before this. In 1781 another traveler wrote,

> *The rabouquin is a triangular piece of board with three strings made of intestines, supported by a bridge, which may be stretched at pleasure by means of pegs, like those of our instruments in Europe; it is indeed nothing else than a guitar with three strings.*[7.]

Three stringed instruments were common, but most of them had six, as well as the characteristic guitar finger board, sound box, and moveable pegs. As guitars have become more available the older instrument has almost disappeared in Africa, but it was clearly an influence on the American musical style. It was even common for performers to press a string against the fingerboard with their chin, a guitar technique still found in some of the mountain areas of the South. Many of the instruments that have survived have hand carved capo d'astros to raise the pitch of the strings. Little is known about the tunings of the ramki, but all of the travelers agree that it was finger picked in repetitive rhythmic patterns. Younger performers in Africa now play a little with a flat pick, but this has come into the music only recently. Many of the American blues singers remember making their own guitars and banjos when they were small children, and the instrument they describe usually has some of the characteristics of the ramki, even to the use of metal pans for the sound box, as was often done in Africa. It may have been that they were helped with the building by a grandmother or a grandfather, whose memory went back to the slavery period when there was still open importation of men, women, and children from Africa.

The strongest American influences on the developing blues were in the area of form, while the most important influence from Africa was on the performance style. African music often is characterized by an elaborately developed rhythmic structure that has continually shifting stress points as the individual performers alter their beat patterns. The blues, generally, is much more oriented to the Euro-American concept of the heavily accented downbeat at the bar line, even though with many of the earlier blues men the bar line emphasis seems to be almost a reluctant afterthought superimposed on a more fluid rhythmic structure. Also the concept of a harmonic structure is less highly developed in African music, and in many of the slave areas two hundred years ago may even have been unknown. Even where there is a use of harmony, the technique is usually limited to parallel harmonies in thirds or fifths with the vocal line. In the blues the harmonic structure is so persistent that the form is often defined by its chord pattern of tonic, subdominant, and dominant relationships. Among the blues singers themselves it is felt that if the piece moves too far from the customary progressions it is no longer a blues, even though it still has many of the other melodic and textual characteristics. Country singers who used open guitar tunings often made only the most perfunctory effort to follow the chord changes of the more or less conventional twelve bar blues form, but they usually sang the harmonic changes, even if they didn't alter the accompaniment figures.

Through the failure of the American academic community to take any interest in the growth of new creative art forms in the United States, it will probably never be possible to determine what musical styles were the dominant influences on the young blues styles. At the point when a few moments conversation with a young singer would have answered nearly all the problems of source and concept there was no one who was interested in either the music or the singers. As late as the 1920's, when the first books were being written on Negro music in the United States, it would have been possible to talk with nearly every major figure in the early blues. Instead the writers spent much of their efforts on the already thoroughly discussed spirituals and made half-hearted efforts to deal with some of the least important areas of local work song. Only John Work, who had earlier noticed the similarities between the African and Afro-American scales, went to a singer. In 1935 he interviewed Gertrude Rainey, who as "Ma" Rainey had been one of the most important of the early women blues singers. [8.] When he talked with her she was still singing, and was staying at a Nashville hotel while her stage show played in the city. She was not able to give him much information, but what she told him does make it clear that the blues form was not generally known throughout the South much before 1900. Her own first memory of the blues was hearing a girl sing a slow, "minor" song in Missouri in 1903, when Ma was singing with a show there. The girl was not from the area, and she had been singing her new kind of songs for the people in the town where the show had stopped. The few local collections of song that were done in Alabama, Louisiana, and Mississippi, don't include a single blues in the fully formed three line stanzaic form, although the emotional attitudes that dominated the later blues were already present.

The pervasive influence of the commercial record business also has made it difficult to untangle the knotted strands of the blues fabric. The first commercially successful recordings were done by young theatre and cabaret entertainers, nearly all of them women, who were working in the larger cities of the North. Their recordings, mostly of songs written for them by professional Negro song writers, were sold everywhere in the South, and when the companies began working with the male singers four or five years later their interest was in ''blues,'' which they usually considered as a twelve-bar, three-line stanza song, like the songs that the girls had recorded. It is clear, from the strength and the variety of the male singing, that the creative impetus in the early blues had been from the country blues men, but the styles had already begun to change by the time these singers were recorded; so the relationships between the blues and closely related forms like the work song and the holler were blurred. The three line verse form was a distinctive poetic form within itself, and as little is known about its line of development from the simple two line rhymes of the work songs. It could have been developed by the singers who improvised their lyrics and found that repeating the first line gave them an additional moment to think of a rhyming line. Although this form was the most widely used there were many variations of the stanza form, from simple two line couplets to complex five and six line verses with involved repetitions of lines and phrases. There was also a compound verse form that developed in the 1930's, which used two lines of more or less recited text, then went back to the sung lines at a slower tempo. The compound verses became especially useful for songs with narrative material and are now used by a number of younger singers. Like the three line stanza, the early forms of the more complex verses are difficult to trace.

Even with the confusion of sources and influences, however, it does seem clear that it was in the Mississippi delta counties that the first blues were sung, and of all the southern areas where the blues became a deeply rooted folk style, it was in the delta where there was the richest creative growth.

MISSISSIPPI

1. MISSISSIPPI

The Mississippi delta is a flat, hot country of straggling lowlands and mounded hills of clay and mud left by the swelling floods of the rivers that meander across its eroded earth. It is an inland delta, the land flooded over by the Yazoo River and the rivers that flow into it from the north, the Tallahatchie and the Sunflower. The rivers wander over the countryside, their banks crude levees of heaped earth and clay, sometimes strengthened near the towns with stones and concrete pilings. The wavering river channels can be followed across the land by the growth of sycamore and poplar left to grow against the levees. Flood control projects have lessened the strength of the spring floods, but the rivers still twist and shift in their beds with the gray rains of late winter and spring.

In the upland pine barrens the soil is streaked with yellow and darkened with the red stain of surface clay. It is poor soil, and its covering is a sparse, meager growth of pine and thin grass. The barrens are lonely and poor, the farm roads only muddy tracks dragging their red clay ruts after them into the stillness of the trees. But on the flat lands near the rivers, the flooding has covered the clay and sand with a heavy layer of topsoil, and the earth is good for cotton. In the long, hot days of late summer the dust from the fields settles over miles of ripening cotton, and the men and mules, even the heavy machines, working the rows are only distant shapes in the haze of the sun. The delta counties, Tunica, Coahoma, Leflore, Sunflower, Yazoo, and Humphreys, are the third largest cotton producing area in the United States, even with a farming system that is still only partially mechanized. The delta counties have a seven month growing season, steady rains in the spring, and the long, hot weeks of July and August, when the clouds drift over the fields with slow indirection and the sun brings the temperature to ninety in the shade as the cotton swells and splits in the gasping air.

Cotton is cruel and demanding in the spring and late summer months; in

25

the spring when the new growth has to be weeded and thinned, and in the fall when it has to be picked. The weeding and thinning goes on for weeks, men working with a hoe, "chopping cotton" up and down the rows, sometimes using a mule or a tractor to drag a cultivator down the soft lines of wavering green stems and leaves. By the end of the summer the plants have dried into a red-brown tangle of spiny stalks, the cotton hanging in its nest of barbs about the level of a man's thigh. For these months the labor in the cotton fields is hard and unending, and for the labor the South, through the century and a half that it has grown cotton, has used Negroes. The delta land was cleared by Negro slave gangs, the fields were leveled and planted, the first cotton picked, ginned, and baled by slaves. When the Civil War ended the system went on almost without change, and the Negro field hand was held to the land with the ruinous "share-crop" system of planting. In 1945 more than sixty percent of Mississippi's farmers were still working as share croppers, and by 1955 the percentage had dropped only to forty-six percent, still the highest in the United States.

Even on the large plantations of the delta, which have become increasingly mechanized, the labor is still done by Negro workers. They live with their families in unpainted shacks along the plantation roads, straggling from plantation to plantation, poorly paid and forced to live under a crude system of paternal semi-slavery. Under the earlier methods of cotton planting so many hands were needed in the fields that for the hundred years between 1840 and 1940 Negroes were in the majority in the state, and in the delta there are still two or three Negroes to every white. Tunica County, a shambling, poor countryside of pine barrens and eroded earth on the Mississippi River below Memphis, has a population that is eighty-one percent Negro, one of the highest percentages of any county in the nation. The only relief for the Negro families caught in the grinding poverty and viciousness of life in rural Mississippi has been flight to the North, and it has been their migration out of the state that has finally given the white population a majority. Between 1950 and 1960 over 325,000 Negroes, out of a Negro population of less than 900,000, fled the state's racism, ignorance, and brutality.

On Saturdays in the small towns of the delta, on a bench near the courthouse or under the trees on one of the side streets, with its old wooden buildings and painted brick store fronts, there is the noise of voices and laughter, shouts as the trucks come in from the plantations and farms and park in front of a store. The courthouse square is crowded with people in to shop, and the trucks and battered farm cars sit along the worn grass of the courthouse park with children waiting impatiently for the adults to get finished and get back to the car. The Negro farmers mingle with the white, their eyes on the ground, looking carefully away when somebody says something to them. They're in faded overalls and work shirts, always with a hat, sometimes in pressed trousers and a white shirt, their wives in shapeless dresses, a handkerchief tied over their hair. Sometimes there are even momentary exchanges between them and a few of the white men, the guarded, uncomfortable effort of the Negro to answer the careless questions of the white man that is sometimes thought of by the white Mississippian as "friendship." But out of the towns, in the rows of farm shacks where the people of the delta live, there is an oppressive isolation. At a rutted cross roads the field workers sit on the ground beside a general store, leaning against the clapboards and the torn advertising posters, wary if a car slows down. If a stranger comes toward a row of shacks at the edge of the stretching fields of new-plowed ground the voices fall silent and a nervous face is pressed against a window in answer to a knock. In the Negro sections of the small towns, the streets unpaved and the sidewalks worn and broken, the men standing in front of a barbership will scatter into the stores and houses if someone unfamiliar walks into the neighborhood.

The music of the delta bears the marks of this separation between the people of the delta. Negroes were more heavily concentrated in the delta than they were in many other areas of the South, and because of the violence of the Mississippi caste system they were kept at an even further distance from the influence of southern white music. With the exception of a few small groups - the people of the sea islands of Georgia and the Carolinas and the families living in the Talladega Forest of Alabama who were so isolated that they retained even fragments of African speech - the delta field hands were less a part of southern life than any other large Negro group. The music that developed in the counties of the delta was so little influenced by American popular music that it was still closely related to the distant African background, and in many ways seemed to be an intense distillation of the slave music that had emerged from the diffuse tribal and cultural influences of the slave society. The delta music had the strength of the work song from which it had only half emerged.

The dominant strains of older music in the delta, the gang work song and the field holler, were entangled with the growing cycles of the cotton crop. The land was cleared by work gangs who felled trees to the rhythm of song leaders, their axes swinging in the light as their voices joined his for the simple responses, grunting as the axe bit into the wood. There were gang songs for chopping, hauling timber, pulling stumps, lifting bales, even for cutting weeds with a hoe. This has long been a characteristic of African music, and it took root throughout the Americas. The mahogany cutters of British Honduras moved their logs through the forests with gang songs and the Bahamas fishermen launched their small sloops with improvised pulling songs. Men sweating under the July sun in a work gang still had the gang songs ringing in their ears when they sang in the cabins at night, and the music of the work songs, with its short vocal phrases, limited melodic range, and insistent rhythm, left its mark on the developing blues style. Sometimes the singers even kept the rhythmic emphasis of the axe fall, pausing before beginning the phrase, and the blues had the feel of the work song, even though the rhythm was usually changed so that the song could be used to accompany dancing.

27

Example 3.

(Axe Song)

Son House (Depot Blues)

Ishman Bracey (Saturday Blues)

The two dominant song forms, the work song and the holler, were distinctly different musical forms, and these differences also found their way into the early delta blues style. A holler is an individual song, and it is very freely structured in its rhythm and its phrasing. It is the song of the man working alone in the fields, musing to himself as he works. Often someone chopping cotton sings a lonely holler, and the plantation mule drivers sing quavering hollers to the animals as they begin work in the first spreading mists of morning. Like the work song, the field holler was closely related to African music, most closely to the praise songs and the individual mens' songs of the West African tribes. The holler left its imprint on the delta blues in the extended vocal phrase, the falsetto voice, the mordent on specific scale tones, and the irregular, embellished cadence.

Example 4.

Holler

The uneasy social line that was drawn between the field hands in their weathered board cabins and the white foremen and townspeople also left the singers to themselves in the development of their vocal scale and the accompaniment rhythm and harmonies. It is difficult to tell how strongly the singers were influenced by the conventional three line blues verse which was used as the first strain to Handy's "St. Louis Blues" in 1914, but the poetic form was widely known. Since Handy found his material in folk sources and spent many of his young years playing with dance orchestras in the delta, the form itself may already have been widespread through the delta, and the conventional blues song of the 1920's may reflect an earlier delta influence - rather than similarities between some delta blues and the conventional popular blues techniques indicating an influence on the Mississippi men. The verse form was generally the three line stanza, but with each singer there was a highly individual approach to the problem of fitting a singing style that was still strongly influenced by its African backgrounds to a harmonic and rhythmic structure that was vaguely derived from standard European harmonic practice. The Mississippi vocal scale was generally a gapped pentatonic, although there were also four and six note groupings. The third of the scale was almost always altered to avoid a clear European major-minor definition. Like most early jazz scales and the folk ragtime scale the modality was mixed, including both major and minor elements, often sounding simultaneously.

Example 5

The third was altered toward either a sharp or flat tonality, depending on its place in the phrase. Although the fourth was generally used, and there was in many of the blues a suggestion of the conventional subdominant harmony in the second line of the verse, it was not a strong tone in the scale and was generally used as an auxiliary to color the third or the fifth in more involved melodic phrases. When the second was used it was generally an auxiliary; although as the delta styles developed in complexity the second became more important through an increasing concern with more sophisticated harmonic patterns. The seventh, in the few scales that it was used, generally had little of the strong leading tone tendency that it has in the European scale, and often seemed to be used an approximation of a harmonic progression to the dominant, where it became the third of the dominant triad.

The African-derived scales, with their strong relationship between the first and fifth tones and their ambiguous use of the third to avoid strong major-minor coloration, dominated the delta blues. It was only with difficulty, however, that they could be fitted to the conventional harmonies of the European guitar; so the accompaniment styles fell back on the older techniques of the rampi, the lyre, and the bow. There was little conventional harmonic movement. Sometimes the guitar was even retuned to an open chord so that it could be played more easily in a repetitive accompaniment ostinato. With the strings tuned to an open E chord or an open G chord there was considerable flexibility in the rhythmic figures that could be picked with the fingers of the right hand, while the left changed the tones to follow the voice. The open E tuning was usually e-b-e'-g-b-e '', a minor tuning, but it was played with one finger on the third string, raising the g to the major g#. Some singers, however, tuned to the major chord, with the g raised the half step. The singer Skip James uses the minor tuning, playing it in major with strong overtones of the minor modality. He calls it "cross-note" tuning because of the crossing between the major and minor during a piece. The G tuning was generally d-g-d'-g'-b-d'', sometimes called the "Spanish" or "slack key" tuning because of the slackening of the lowest e string down a whole step to d. It is a major tuning, and it was usually played with the strings open, sometimes even with the guitar flat across the singer's lap. It had a darker sound than the E tuning because of the lowering of the bass string to the fifth of the key. The cadential V-I used the lowest strings of the guitar, and descending bass lines could move down the lowest string from the tonic G to the dominant D. Charley Patton often used this tuning, pulling the bass string with a strong slapping sound on the descending line. There was a tuning in open D-d-a-d-g-b-d''. and the standard guitar tuning was used as well, the e-a-d-g-b-e' European tuning, sometimes called "minor" tuning or "the key of minor" in the delta. With all the tunings, however, the guitar was usually as much as a fourth below standard concert pitch. It was difficult to change chords in the open tunings, except by barring across at the fifth fret for the subdominant or the seventh fret for the dominant, but the blues of the delta were dominated by the voice and the rhythmic pattern, and the harmonic style was less intensively developed.

In a few of the blues there was no harmonic change, and there was not even an effort to follow the movement of the vocal line with accompaniment figures in the guitar. Instead the singer picked an ostinato pattern over and over in the guitar and sang against it in an elaborately developed melodic structure that was only loosely tied to the rhythm of the accompaniment. This style was closely related to the African music of the slave coast, in which accompaniment instruments repeated a simple figure over and over while the chanted melody was sung against it. Although the style was musically limited there was considerable variety within the repetitive patterns. Closely tied to these styles were accompaniments which combined the ostinato patterns with an effort to sketch in the more conventional blues harmonies. In these accompaniments the guitar played an insistent note or an open chord under the vocal phrase; then followed the voice with an ostinato figure. These accompaniments became almost a characteristic of the delta style, even though they forced the singers into irregular rhythmic patterns. If the vocal phrase ended in the middle of a measure and then was followed by a four beat accompaniment figure, as many of the patterns were, then the blues line became an uneasy phrase of irregular measure length. Often the singers simply adjusted to the irregularity, rather than trying to alter their accompaniment, and many blues have measures of 5/4 and 6/4 between the standard 4/4 measures. There was also a wide use of a half measure of 2/4 within the vocal line to introduce the sung phrase of four measures of 4/4 rhythm.

One of the dominant characteristics of the delta accompaniment style was the use of the guitar to play a melodic unison, or near unison, with the voice. It was so strongly tied to the early delta style that singers can often be placed by the extent of the melodic doubling between the voice and the guitar. Often these lines were finger picked, as part of the more complex ostinato patterns. Charley Patton, in pieces like "Down The Dirt Road Blues," used this finger picked melody in 8th notes against the reiterated fundamental tone in the lower strings. The guitar, however, was limited by its metal frets to tones that were more or less within the diatonic framework of a European guitar style. The singer could alter the tones to some extent by "choking" the string, (pushing it to one side on the finger board to raise the pitch), but this was difficult to do for a more extended melodic line. In part because of this melodic limitation and in part because of the distinctiveness of the sound, many Mississippi singers used a bottleneck or metal ring on the third or fourth finger of the left hand. With this they were able to play a melodic line that followed the voice very closely, even when the vocal line used tones that were within the pentatonic scale framework. This unison melody played with a slide of some kind and a bass line of alternating root and fifth tones played with the thumb became widespread among the delta singers.

The vocal style of the delta was hard and unrelenting; the voice usually heavy, the tone produced at the back of the throat with rougher growling tones, and the falsetto voice used for contrast or emotional emphasis. Often the melodic range was limited to a few notes within a partial octave, probably from the long hours on the work gangs, where melodies were kept as simple as possible so that they could be sung over and over and still leave enough breath to use an axe or a pick. A few singers, among them Robert Johnson and Skip James, used some vocal embellishment, and scale tones were used with some flexibility within the phrase, but the usual melodic movement was in intervals of a third or a fourth, and the tones were clearly focused. It was generally in the blues with a field holler background that there was more use of the mordent and the embellished cadence.

It is difficult to find traces of the earliest blues styles, but it was in the delta, in Cleveland, Mississippi, that W. C. Handy heard a man singing a blues in 1895. It is the earliest moment at which someone remembers hearing the blues in the South, and it could have been in the delta that the blues finally emerged as a musical style distinct from the field holler and the gang song of the rest of the rural South. There was the heavy concentration of Negro field workers, an almost complete isolation from the white society, and a strongly developed tradition of rhymed work song material; all of these are factors that could have led to the growth of a distinctive musical style. The roots of the delta blues, with their half remembered elements of African song and the work rhythms of the years of slavery, go as deep within the singers as the roots of the cotton in the hot, dusty fields go deep within the delta soil.

Without the phonograph record the blues styles of the Mississippi delta would have been only a vaguely remembered sound, like a bird's whistle across the fields in the sun. Fortunately, however, many of the singers were able to record. With the move out of Mississippi by many younger Negro families in the years after the first World War there was a market in the northern slums for the music from "down home," and the companies found a strong musical tradition when they began looking for

32

local blues singers. Victor Records, with a field unit in Memphis set up by Ralph Peer, recorded a number of important singers in the late 1920's, and Paramount Records, through their talent scout, H. C. Spears in Jackson, brought some of the most creative singers up to the studios in Grafton, Wisconsin. Columbia did little work in the area, but there were delta singers among others on Brunswick, Gennett and OKeh labels. The great delta folk blues artist, John Hurt, recorded for OKeh in Memphis, then again in New York in 1928. In the 1930's there was continued interest in the delta music and the American Recording Corporation, Vocalion Records, and the Bluebird label of R.C.A. Victor used delta singers for considerable material. The amount of Mississippi music recorded before the second World War was very large, and it included some of the most creative blues to be recorded during the late 'twenties and the 'thirties. Some important Mississippi singers were probably missed by the companies, whose interest in the music was only sporadic, but from the reminiscences of some of the older singers it would seem that most of the dominant figures in the development of the delta style were recorded, and some of them extensively. Of the dozens of singers to be recorded a handful have already emerged as among the most significant artists that the blues has produced, among them men like Charley Patton, Son House, Skip James, Robert Johnson, and Booker White, who seem to represent the musical tradition which shaped them, and was in turn shaped by their own creative expression.

33

2. CHARLEY PATTON

The delta blues grew out of the earth of the delta countryside, but the same piece of ground can grow ragweed, mullien, jack pine, field grass, or black-eyed daisies. A developing art form grows like the weeds beside a road, dozens of styles growing together until one crowds aside the others with its strength and vitality. In the early period of growth in the music of the delta it was Charley Patton, from a farm outside of Edwards in Hinds County, who left the deepest impression on its blues. As a younger singer, Booker White, remembered,[1]

> *I always wanted to be like old Charley Patton, long time ago when I was a kid out here, and play them numbers about "Hitch up my buggy and saddle up my black mare," and I used to pick cotton and come around in Clarksdale there to them cafes and things eating cheese and cracker - none of the other boys, they didn't have any idea what I was thinking about - I'd say I wants to come to be a great man like Charley Patton, but I didn't want to be killed like he did, the way he had to go. I've always realized I knew I had to die, but I didn't want one of them old sandfoot womens coming up and cut my throat or do something to me that's unnecessary. I tell you the truth the first drink of whiskey that I ever drinken, Charley Patton gave me a little in a spoon. He said, "You're too young to drink too much of whiskey, but I'm going to give you enough to know what it's about." And I still think about that. I wish I'd asked him to give me the spoon... I just wish today I could shake Charley Patton's hand...*

Charley was a small man, short and slight with a thin face and soft, wavy hair, but he has left a long shadow in the memories of people in the delta who heard him sing. In August, 1963, two men trying to follow the threads of Charley's life, Gayle Dean Wardlow, a young white Mississippian who was living in Jackson, and Bernard Klatzko, an accountant from Long Island, found that despite the thirty years that had passed since Charley's death he was still remembered by most of the people living in the sections of the countryside where he had played. Gayle had learned a few months before that Patton had died on Dockery's Plantation, outside of Cleveland, Mississippi, in Sunflower County. As Klatzko later described their trip,[2.]

... We entered Sunflower County ... three miles from the County line we stopped at a general store -- all there was of the town of Dockery. Out beyond the general store and to its right, there was this big blue sign over an entranceway to a large plantation. Its white lettering read: WILL DOCKERY AND SON JOS. DOCKERY.

We drove in, passed some farm machinery and a cotton gin and came upon a vast, beautifully tended cotton field. However, we turned our attention to a row of Negro houses that stood opposite the field. At the first house a middle age woman answered our knock on the screen.

"Did you ever hear of Charley Patton?" I started off.

"Charley Patton? He's dead."

"Did you know him?"

"No. I only moved here about 10 years ago. Why don't you ask some people who have lived here a long time. You can find them on the other end." She said this pointing to the other group of houses which lay to the left of the entrance road; we had turned right on entering...

The next few inquiries proved very fruitful. At the first house, a young woman directed us to her father-in-law, Johnny Wilder, who ran the gasoline pump in front of the general store and who had known Patton well. In the next house, dwelt Patton's cousin, who directed us to the machine shop where Tom Cannon, Patton's nephew, worked. Sure, he remembered his uncle, but didn't know too much about him. "Why don't you ask my mother, Viola Cannon? That's Charley's sister. She can tell you all about him. She lives in Cleveland." We went back to the general store and bought Johnny Wilder and ourselves bottles of Coke and sat on a bench in the shade. It was another blistering hot day.

Johnny Wilder was brown and lean, of medium height and grey-headed. He was most amiable but I detected an air of uneasiness about him when we started to ply him with questions. "Charley Patton was living here when I came here back in 1917. He traveled all around but always came back to

35

Dockery's. Then a few years later, he left for good. Mr. Jed fired him."

"What songs did he sing?" Were there any other blues singers on the plantation?"

"He sang 'Hitch up my pony/Saddle up my grey mare' and 'What you want with a rooster...' As for other singers, there was Son House on Dockery's at the same time. He came from Drew, and Nathan Bank, also from Drew, played with them. There was Willie Brown, too. They all played for picnics and jook joints."

"Patton sang about Tom Rushen. Did you ever hear of him?" I asked.

"Tom Rushen is Iry Rushen's brother," said Johnny. "Iry Rushen was Will Dockery's bookkeeper. He just died recently."

With that, we left for Cleveland to find Viola Cannon. After several inquiries we were directed to the "new" houses. We arrived at a street of comparatively new frame, one-story, painted homes, but no larger than the unpainted variety. A man we enlisted for further help pointed to Viola's house and added that if we wanted to know more about Patton we should ask Millie Toy. She had been married to Patton and now lived in Boyle. Viola came to the door. She was about five foot five, very lean, unsmiling, proud and seemed a little disturbed by the intrusion. She had yellow brown skin, and a long lean face with strong, regular features.

"Charley was a great blues singer" she said. "He taught them all, Howlin' Wolfe, Willie Brown, Son House. He made up all the songs himself. He followed a guitar player around Dockery's as a boy. I forgot the guitar player's name, but Charley didn't learn any singing from him. Charley made up his own singing."

"Where was Charley born?" Gayle asked.

"He was born on a farm outside Edwards in 1887. He had two brothers, William and Will C. and two sisters, Katie and myself. All are dead. I'm the last. We moved from Edwards to Dockery's when Charley was still a young boy. He didn't start to play guitar until we were on Dockery's. My father was a very big man and my mother was short and real good-looking with long, straight hair. Charley himself wasn't too big and he was thin."

"Was Charley religious?" I asked.

36

Viola chuckled and said, "No, he wasn't religious."

"Then how did he learn all those religious songs and why did he sing them?"

I felt a little embarrassed asking that question.

"My father was the elder of a church on the plantation. Charley knew all those religious songs from boyhood and sang them later 'cause they're good songs, I guess."

"Did you ever hear of Minnie Franklin?" asked Gayle.

"Well, Charley's first wife was named Gertrude. He met Minnie Franklin in Merigold in 1921 right after he left Dockery's. Then, he followed her on down to Vicksburg after his best gun and money." Viola recalled this incident with fits of laughter.

"Where did Charley do most of his playing?" I interjected.

"Charley played all over. He traveled with medicine shows and played with Blind Lemon," she replied.

"Did Charley drink much?" I wanted to know.

"No. He hardly drank at all..."

A delta singer who had left to live in St. Louis in 1925, J. D. Short, remembered meeting Charley when he was a young man.[3.]

"He used to play the guitar and he'd make the guitar say, 'Lord have mercy, Lord have mercy, Lord have mercy, pray, brother, pray, save poor me.' Now that's what Charley Patton'd make the guitar say."

J. D. was quiet, dark man who struggled against the difficulties of St. Louis slum life with a gentle good nature. He was able to fill in a little of the life that Patton had led when he was in his twenties. J. D. met Charley,

... out on little Mirthy Bow from Hollandale, Mississippi ... he was doing some logging out in there, hauling logs, hauling timber and stuff out in there ... that's mostly what he did. He mostly followed timber camps and levee camps and stuff like that ... he always kept a guitar, but he didn't usually carry it with him. He would come along driving a wagon or something back in them days and somebody had a guitar around playing and he wasn't in a hurry he'd just stop by and play the guitar some and let the people hear him.

As they drove across the Mississippi cotton counties looking for Patton's last wife, Bertha Lee, Wardlow and Klatzko found that the mention of Charley's name usually brought a response like J.D.'s - a memory of Patton as the singer and entertainer.[4]

To the people who lived with him, and to his friends, Charley was a small, intense, fretful man who blustered his way out of fights, sang with fierce strength, and survived as best he could in a violent countryside. Son House, who met Patton in 1930, remembers going back to Bertha Lee after he and Charley had been out on a two day drunk, and he heard them arguing in the next room; then there was a crash and he heard Charley saying, "I told you not to get me angry." Then he heard more sounds of a fight and a louder crash and Charley called out to Son to come in and help. Bertha Lee was bigger than Charley and she had him down on the floor. "Son," Charley said, "Get this woman away from me before I hurt her." Son told Julius Lester, who talked with him in New York in 1964, of another time he and Willie Brown found Charley getting out of a fight.[5]

> *I remember one night Willie and I and Charlie were to play at the same place and Willie and I were late, but Charlie had gotten there kind of early. And the guys got off the center kind of early, too. Got to fighting and shooting off those old owl-head pistols. Well, Willie and I got near to the house and we heard such a gruntin' and a rattlin' coming up through the stalks, and I said, "Wait a minute, Willie. Hold it. I hear something coming up through the cotton field. Don't you hear it?" He said, "Yeah. It's something." We were always suspicious, you know, about animals. Out in the country around there, it wouldn't be anything to see a teddy-bear or something. So we got the idea we wanted to hurry up and get to the road where we could see it. Finally, who should pop out to the roadside but Charlie! He looked and saw us and said, "I'll kill 'em all. I'll kill 'em all." Me and Willie started laughing and told him, "How you gon' kill 'em all? We heard you running."*

Patton's music was as much a part of the delta as the mud on the banks of the Sunflower River or the smell of the fields back of Belzoni. He sang in cabins, in ramshackle road houses, in country dance halls, even in gardens and plantation house back yards. He sang for everybody in the delta, white and colored, and he had songs for every kind of audience. Nearly half of the songs that he recorded were play party songs or folk songs, country ballads or gospel songs. He could be thought of almost as a songster, rather than a blues singer, but songsters usually learn their blues from other singers. His blues were among the most compelling and individual of the early blues period. And for once recordings seem to represent a singer at his best. Son House has said that when Charley performed for audiences he was always playing with his guitar behind his head or doing a little dance as he sang, and that his recordings were

38

much better than Charley's singing was in person. A delta singer of Patton's generation, Babe Stovall, who was found in Meridian, Mississippi, by a New Orleans art dealer named Larry Borenstein, still ends his performances playing the guitar behind his head or behind his back, and the effect is a little confused musically, although the sight of Babe standing in a New Orleans patio with his Virginia Military Institute overcoat hanging down to his ankles, and his steel-bodied National guitar sitting on top of his head while he plays a guitar solo, is difficult to forget. Patton, with his rough voice and his heavy guitar accompaniments, must have had the same effect when he stood up in a dimly lit road house to do one of this songs.

Many of Charley's blues had deep roots in the delta. He was one of the most "local" singers even of the early period, when there was considerable mention of local towns and counties in the blues. He seems to have known every small town and plantation and sheriff and bootlegger within fifty miles of his cabin - and to have been unconcerned with much that was happening anywhere else. Some of the most difficult passages to understand in his blues often turn out to be the names of people in the area, or of the small towns of the country side. In "Tom Rushen Blues" it was Mr. Holloway, Mr. Day, sheriff of Bolivar County, and the sheriff who followed him into office, Tom Rushen.

I lay down last night, thought that I would have my peace, (sleep?)
umhuh,
I lay down last night, thought that I would have my peace, (sleep?)
umhuh,
But when I woke up Tom Rushen was shaking me.

When you get in trouble there's no use to screamin'
and cryin', umhuh,
When you get in trouble there's no use to screamin'
and cryin', umhuh,
Tom Rushen will take you back to prison now flyin'.

It was late one night, Holloway was gone to bed, umhuh.
It was late one night, Holloway was gone to bed, umhuh.
Mr. Day brought whiskey ('til he dropped under) Holloway's head.

Well, boozie booze, lord, to carry me through.
It take booly booze lord, to carry me through.
Well, the days seem like years in the jailhouse where there is
no booze.

Got up this morning Tom Day was standin' 'round, umhuh.
Got up this morning Tom Day was standin' 'round, umhuh.
If he lose his office now he runnin' from town to town.

Let me tell you folkses just how he treated me, umhuh,
I'm gon' tell you folkses just how he treated me, umhuh.
Lord, he caught me an' I was drunk as I could be.

In "High Sheriff Blues" he sang about Belzoni, in Humphreys County, its sheriff, Mr. Ware, and Mr. Purvis, who seems to have been a local landowner.

> When the trial's in Belzoni, ain't no use screamin' and cryin',
> umhuh,
> When the trial's in Belzoni, ain't no use to scream and cry,
> umhuh,
> Mr. Ware will take you back to Belzoni jail house umhuh,
> (for life?)
>
> Let me tell you folkses, how he treated me, umhuh,
> Let me tell you folkses, how he treated me, umhuh,
> And he put me in a cellar just as dark as it could be.
>
> It was late one evening Mr. Purvis was standin' 'round,
> umhuh,
> It was late one evening Mr. Purvis was standin' 'round,
> umhuh,
> Mr. Purvis told Mr. Webb, sir, to let poor Charley down.
>
> It takes boozey booze, lord, to carry me through, umhuh,
> It takes booley boo, lord, to carry me through, umhuh,
> (Mr. Purvis...)   jailhouse where there is no booze.
>
> I got up one morning feeling awful mm, umhuh,
> I got up one morning feeling mighty bad, umhuh,
> It must not a been the Belzoni jail I had - blues I had, boy.
>
> While I was in trouble you know no use to scream and cry,
> umhuh,
> When I was in prison ain't no use to scream and cry.
> Mr. Purvis on his mansion, he just don't pay no mind.

Charley's longest blues about the delta was his song about the floods of 1927, "High Water Everywhere, Part 1 and 2." The verses conveyed a strong impression of the flood waters that streamed over the bottom land during the worst days of flooding. (This piece is also one of Patton's most difficult to understand, but Don Kent, a Patton enthusiast living in Chicago, after several months work has succeeded in transcribing all of the verses, and it is his transcription which follows.) The spoken comments were probably by Willie Brown.

> Part 1. The back water done rose, sir, an' tumbled down,
> drove me down the line.
> Back water done rolled and tumbled, drove poor Charley
> down the line.
>
> An' I tell the world the water done struck through this town.

Lord, the whole roun' country, Lord, river is overflowin'.
Lord, the whole roun' country, man, it's overflowed.
   Spoken: You know I can't stay here; I'm boun' to go where
        it's high, boy.
I would go to the hill country, but they got me barred.

Now, look a here now, Lelah, river risin' high.
Look here, boys (   ) leave it to me, river is ragin' high.
   Spoken: Boy, it's risin' over there, yeah.
I'm gonna move over to Greensboro, 'fore I take (a good) bye.

Look a here, water now, Lordy, 'sup rol-rolled
   'most everywhere.
The water at Greenville, Lord, it done rose everywhere.
   Spoken: Boy, you can't never stay here.
I would go down to Rosedale, but they tell me
   there's water there.

Now, the water now, mama, done struck Charley's town.
Well, they tell me the water done struck Charley's town.
   Spoken: Boy, I'm going to Vicksburg.
Well, I'm goin' to Vicksburg on that high o' mine.

I am goin' on dry water where land don't never flow.
Well, I'm goin' on a hill where water, water don't never flow.
   Spoken: Boy, (hit Sharkey County and everything slid
      down in Stover.)
But I'll count the water isn't over in Tallahassie, sho'.
   Spoken: Boy, go way for Tallahassie, find it over there.

Lord, the water done rushed all...that 'ol Jackson road.
Lord, the water done reached over the Jackson road.
   Spoken: Boy, it got my car.
I'm goin' back to the hilly country, won't be worried no mo'.

Part 2. Back water at Blytheville, backed up all around.
Back water at Blytheville, done took Joiner town.
It was fifty families and children, some left dead and drowned.

The water was risin', up in my friend's door.
The water was risin', up in my friend's door.
The man said to his women folk, "Lord, we'd better go."

The water was risin', got up in my bed.
Lord, the water is rollin', up in my friend's door.
I thought I would take a trip, Lord, out on the big ice sled.

41

Awwwuhhnn I hear the water, Lord, roll above my door.

Spoken: Low water...look a here.
I hear (it risin', Lord, Loring) sinkin' down.
I couldn't get no boat ride, left me sink on down.

Ooooh-ahh the water risin', families sinkin' down.
Say, now, the water was risin', airplanes is all aroun'.
Spoken: The water is all aroun'.
It was fifty men and children, come to sink an' drown.

Ooooh - uuhhnn Lordy, women and grown men down.
Oooh-uhhh, women and children sinkin' down.
Spoken: Lord have mercy, uh.
I couldn't see nobody home an' was no one to be found.

He usually used the conventional three line verse in his blues compositions. The folk and country dance songs that he recorded he generally
left in their original form. He sometimes varied the verse form within
a blues, repeating the last few words of the first line except for the
final word, with which he ended the last repetition. In "Moon Going
Down" he began,

Oh the moon goin' down, babe, sun's about to shine.
Oh the moon goin' down, babe, sun's about to shine.
(Henrietta) told me, lord, don't want you hangin' 'round.

and by the fifth verse he had extended the first line to,

'Cause the smoke stack's black an' the bell it shine like -
                                        bell it shine like -
                                        bell it shine like gold,
'Cause the smoke stack's black an' the bell it shine like gold.
Lord I ain't gonna walk there, can't get 'round no mo'.

It was not an original device with Patton, but he used it with considerable
skill to heighten the tension of his best performances. He also knew a
number of songs which came from the older country traditions. His
version of the boll weevil ballad, "Mississippi Boll Weevil Blues," was
an archaic dance song with only a single musical phrase which repeated
over and over.

Example 6

The sketchy "ballad" used verses of a few words each, some of the phrases not even complete as he used the guitar to end the line.

He's a little Bo Weevil keeps movin'a in the ... lordy ...
You can plant your cotton and you won't get half a cent, lordy ...
Boweevil, Boweevil, where's your little home? Lordy ...

It could have been a song like "Boll Weevil" that W. C. Handy heard in Cleveland, Mississippi, around the turn of the century and described as "... one of those over-and-over strains that seemed to have no very clear beginning and certainly no ending at all. The strumming attained a disturbing monotony, but on and on it went...." At a cabin buck dance a song like "Mississippi Boll Weevil" usually goes on until the dancers are too tired to keep up or the singer has run out of words. The singer Handy heard could even have been Patton, who was then a young man living and beginning to play in Cleveland.

Another of the blues that had the feel of the older field traditions was "When Your Way Gets Dark," a brooding composition that used lines from prison work songs almost as a single line verse. The vocal phrase was followed by a set melodic pattern in the guitar; then there was a cadential line that drew on Charley's usual final verse rhymes. His other blues often used conventional verses in haphazard arrangements, but in all of them there were moments, lines, phrases, entire verses, that were tied to Charley Patton's life in the Mississippi delta before the 1930's.

The delta haze hangs over some of Charley's years of wandering and singing, but it is possible to sketch in a few of the details for a rough portrait. He was born, as his sister said, on a farm outside of Edwards in 1887, and his family moved to Dockery's when he was still a boy. He grew up there, learned to play the guitar a little and began singing. His first wife was a girl named Gertrude; in 1908 he married Minnie Toy. He stayed on at Dockery's as a field hand and wagon driver until the early 1920's when he was fired. He went to Merigold and met Minnie Franklin and lived with her, probably in Vicksburg, for a year or so. About 1924 or 1925 he came back to Merigold with a woman named Sudy and lived with her "...near Pimbles Ferry on the other side of the Sunflower River," as Sam Manifield remembered. Charley drifted in and out of most of the delta towns as well, although he doesn't seem to have gone out of the state for any length of time. In 1929 he was in Jackson for a few months, and during these months Charley Patton, the delta blues man and songster, brushed against the outside world of American popular music.

In the late 1920's Paramount Records, a Chicago company which had been very successful in selling blues to the new urban Negro market, was making an effort to find singers who were still living in southern rural areas. The company had made an arrangement with a man named H. C. Spears, who had a music store on North Farrow Street in Jackson, to do tests of anyone he thought might sell some records in the area. Thanks to Spears, Paramount left behind what is probably the most important collection of blues material ever to be recorded in the United States. Spears sent Patton on to Arthur Laibley, who was one of the recording directors for Paramount, and Charley did his first recordings at Richmond, Indiana, in the old Gennett Record Studios, on Friday, June 14, 1929. He was in Indiana only long enough for the sessions and went back to Jackson when he had finished recording. Six weeks later, on July 27, 1929, his first release was advertised in the Chicago *Defender*.

PONY BLUES
by Charley Patton

Here is a hot record by the one and only Charley Patton - a new Paramount artist - one of the best known singers and guitar players in the South. What he can't do with a guitar ain't worth mentioning. He starts off for Paramount with a bang - with Record No. 12792, "Pony Blues"...

At almost the same time Paramount issued one of Charley's religious songs, "Prayer of Death" - actually one side was "Prayer of Death" and the other side was an alternate take of "I'm Going Home" - on Paramount 12799, under the name Elder J. J. Hadley. Charley's religious singing was almost as exciting as his blues singing, but Paramount was probably trying to circumvent the usual reluctance country people felt at buying religious records performed by a blues artist. The blues release, "Pony Blues," was a song that Charley had been singing around the delta for years, and there must have been some response to the record. Paramount brought him up for three more sessions during the next thirteen months and even made an effort to advertise his new releases. Booker White remembered that he couldn't "fit into a room" in Clarksdale when Charley's newest record was being played. For the second advertisement Paramount made an effort to sell Charley as a "Masked Marvel," and on September 14, 1929, the Chicago *Defender* had a drawing of a sophisticated looking man in evening clothes wearing a mask, with the words, "Who sings this great new Paramount Record? Who is the Masked Marvel?..." The record was Paramount 12805, "Screamin' And Hollerin' The Blues" and "Mississippi Bo Weevil Blues." The picture must have surprised the "Masked Marvel," if he ever saw it.

Early in 1930 Charley was living in Lula, a small town off Highway 61 in Coahoma County, north of Clarksdale, and in Lula he met both Son House and Bertha Lee, the woman who lived with him until he died four years later. As Son remembers,[6.]

"PONY BLUES"

by Charley Patton

HERE is a hot record by the one and only Charley Patton — a new Paramount artist — one of the best known singers and guitar players in the South. What he can't do with a guitar ain't worth mentioning. He starts off for Paramount with a Bang — with Record No. 12792, "Pony Blues". Be sure and get it from your dealer, or send us the coupon.

[**12792—Pony Blues** and **Banty Rooster Blues,**]
Charley Patton and His Guitar.

12791—Sing Song Blues and **Smiling Blues,** Jack O'Diamonds; Guitar acc. by Bob Coleman.

12790—Fetch Your Water and **Seen This Morning Blues,** Charlie Spand and Guitar; piano acc.

12768—Gutter Man Blues and **Wobblin'** in the Mud, Geo. Hannah; instrumental acc.

12773—Bucket Of Blood and **Playing The Dozen**—Piano Solos by Will Ezell.

12714—Selling That Stuff and **Beedle Um Bum,** The Hokum Boys; Piano-Guitar acc.

12771—Oil Well Blues and **Saturday Night Spender Blues,** Blind Lemon Jefferson and His Guitar.

12758—Wasn't That Doggin' Me and **Rockin' On The Hill Blues,** Beale Street Sheiks and Guitars.

Sacred Numbers

12766—How It Is With Me and **I Want To Know Will He Welcome Me There,** Norfolk Jubilee Quartette.

12680—His Eye Is On The Sparrow and **I Wouldn't Mind Dying If Dying Was All,** Norfolk Jubilee Quartette.

SEND NO MONEY! If your dealer is out of the records you want, send us the coupon below. Pay postman 75 cents for each record, plus small C. O. D. fee when he delivers records. We pay postage on shipments of two or more records.

Paramount
The Popular Race Record
ELECTRICALLY RECORDED

The New York Recording Laboratories
Port Washington, Wis.

Send me the records checked (✓) below 75 cents each.

{ } 12792 { } 12791 { } 12790
{ } 12798 { } 12773 { } 12714
( ) 12771 { } 12758 { } 12765 { } 12680

Name..............................
Address..........................
City .... State............

CHARLEY PATTON ADVERTISEMENT

CHARLEY PATTON ADVERTISEMENT

"I went up to Lula to see my aunt, and being up there, I heard that that was where Charlie Patton lived. I'd heard of him, heard a lot of his records, so I made myself acquainted with him. I knew a little more about him than he did me. Now Willie Brown, he was living up on Robinsonville, and he and Charlie Patton had known one another for years. They'd gotten together out on a white man's place they call the Dockery Plantation. It's way down and out from Ruleville -- somewhere down in there."

Charley had already brought another friend, a fiddler and singer named Henry Sims, from Farrell, Mississippi, as well as a second guitarist and "commentor," who was probably Willie Brown, for sessions late in 1929. For his session in July, 1930, he brought up Willie and Son, as well as a girl, Louise Johnson, who was from Willie's town of Robinsonville. The music from these sessions is one of the most significant group of delta blues to be recorded, and it is possible to hear in each of the other singers as well an influence from the voice and personality of Charley Patton.

The delta soil that produced Charley, Willie and Son left its dust on all of them, but each of them was strongly individual. They all spoke with a delta accent, but each of them spoke in his own manner. Charley's was a heavier voice than the others, heavier and stronger despite his small size. His accompaniment style was as intense as his singing. In his blues he used a number of scales, with the pentatonic forms predominating, although in his folk songs and gospel pieces the scale was often the European diatonic. For his most personal blues he used melodies which became distinctive with him, although they may be older songs that he altered for his own use. Without earlier recordings or field transcriptions it will always be impossible to tell with any certainty the sources of the delta blues that were recorded in the late twenties. The melody he used most frequently was a repetitive pattern of only four notes, and may have been derived from an older field song.

Example 7

(High Water Everywhere)

♩ = 132

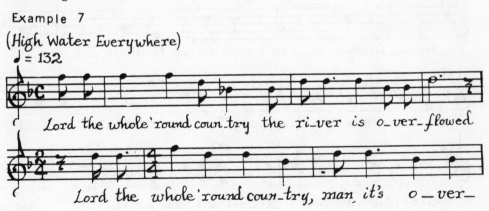

Lord the whole 'round coun-try the ri-ver is o-ver-flowed

Lord the whole 'round coun-try, man it's o-ver-

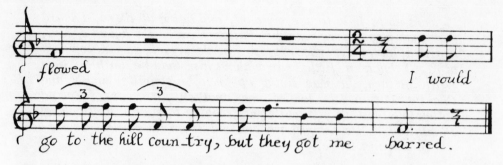

flowed   I would

go to the hill coun_try, but they got me   barred.

His accompaniments for the melody varied considerably, but there was usually an ostinato in an 8/8 rhythm for the first line, which resolved with more or less confusion to one of his less difficult accompaniment patterns in 4/4 for the rest of the verse. He used this melody for several blues, among them "High Water Everywhere," "Moon Going Down," "Bird Nest Bound," "Revenue Man Blues," "Jersey Bull Blues," "Screamin' And Hollerin' The Blues," "Love Is My Stuff," "Rattlesnake Blues," and "Heart Like Railroad Steel." The other melody which was distinctive with Patton was the ballad-like melody that he used for the two narrative blues about his prison experiences, "Tom Rushen Blues" and "High Sheriff Blues." The scale was close to a European diatonic in its use of the second, not only as an upper auxiliary in measure 2, but as a passing tone in measure 8. Usually Patton moved his melodic line by disjunct intervals of at least a third, but in both these blues the angularity of his line was softened by the use of the second and sixth of the scale. The vocal line ended on the fifth of the scale- e in the key of A - in both of the opening two lines; so Patton reinforced the tonic A by humming a c# - a to end the phrase.

Example 8
(High Sheriff Blues)
♩=110

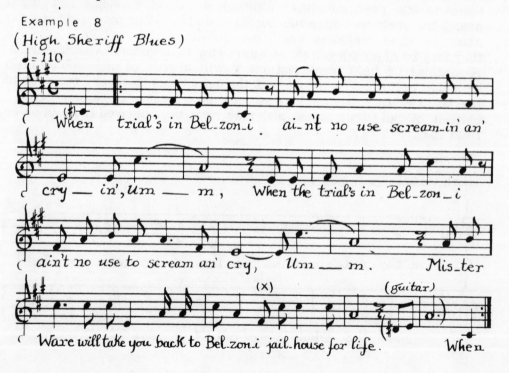

When   trial's in Bel_zon_i   ai_n't no use scream_in an'

cry — in', Um — m,   When the trial's in Bel_zon _i

ain't no use to scream an' cry,   Um — m.   Mis_ter

(X)   (guitar)

Ware will take you back to Bel_zon_i jail_house for life.   When

50

For other blues he often used melodies that were widely known throughout the Mississippi and Tennessee area. The Memphis medicine show singers were in the delta every summer, and they left as many melodies behind them as they picked up for their own use. The melody which Patton used for "It Won't Be Long" and "Banty Rooster Blues" was the melody known in Memphis as "Brownsville Blues," and used by a number of singers in that area. "Banty Rooster Blues" may have been derived from a 1927 recording made in Texas by Walter Rhodes, "The Crowing Rooster," but it seems more probable that both of them learned the song from an earlier source which is still untraced. Patton's "Going To Move To Alabama," - derived from Jim Jackson's "Kansas City Blues" - is one of the few songs which can be tied to a direct source. "Elder Green Blues" also used one of the widely known melodies, the "Don't You Leave Me Here" melody, which early became part of the developing musical vocabulary of instrumental jazz. Although many of his other songs came from either work gang chants or religious hymns, he used little vocal embellishment, centering the tone directly on the note and limiting himself to occasional portmenti, descending sliding tones on notes ending his verses. The voice itself was very dark and forced, with an almost harsh tone.

The blues is a loose form which is thought of by most blues singers as an expression of words or emotion rather than musical complexity, and the melodic rhythms have almost always been dictated by the text of the verse. Patton kept in many of his blues, like the vestigial tail of a spring tadpole in the mud of the Sunflower River, the irregular rhythmic pattern of a spontaneous work song. In these blues the accompaniment phrase between the lines was shortened and the first words of the vocal phrase became a half measure, almost always in 2/4. The usual rhythmic pattern for the verse was 2/4 - 4/4 - 4/4 - 4/4 - 4/4 - 2/4 - 4/4 - 4/4 4/4 - 4/4 - 2/4 - 4/4 - 4/4 - 4/4 - 4/4. It was an awkward form, but it was an effective variant on the more conventional blues forms.

Example 9

In his accompaniments he used E and G tunings, as well as the conventional "minor" tuning. For some of his songs, among them "Pony Blues" and the "Moon Going Down" group, the accompaniment was built on tonic harmony in ostinato patterns, but for most of his blues and for many of the hymns and folk songs, he played a melodic line in near unison with the voice and picked a bass line with his thumb. The bass line usually alternated between the lowest tonic and the octave or the fifth above it.

Several of the blues were finger picked, among them "Down The Dirt Road Blues" and "Elder Green Blues." He still used a melodic line which closely followed his voice, and to sustain the guitar note he usually played in doubled 8th note patterns. Often the interplay between the vocal rhythm and the guitar rhythm in this style was highly complex, and he also used hesitations - following a note in the guitar with a short figure in the voice - in several of the pieces. Most often, however, he used a knife or a bottleneck to play a melodic line that was closer to the altered scale of the voice. "Banty Rooster Blues," "Tom Rushen Blues," "Hammer Blues," and most of the religious songs were played in this style, with the thumb reiterating an insistent bass line in the lower strings of the guitar. In the open E tuning he limited himself to a suggestion of harmonic change in his blues, but in religious songs like "I'm Going Home", he barred at the fifth fret for the subdominant chord. In the G tuning he was able to outline the I - IV - V blues harmonic patterns, and in the conventional tuning he had some skill in more elaborate chord progressions. In his performance of "A Spoonful," an old country song that Paramount labeled "Spoonful Blues," he even developed an accompaniment in an embryonic VI - II - V - I progression. There was, however, an earlier recording of the song by Papa Charlie Jackson, "All I Want Is A Spoonful," and this harmonic progression was a characteristic of Jackson's style; so Patton's recording may have been influenced by Jackson's performance five years earlier.

The largest group of songs other than blues that Charley left on record were religious. As his sister remembered he learned them from his father when he was still a boy. Many of the performances, especially the "Prayer of Death" and the duet with Bertha Lee, "Oh Death," were as harsh and searing as his blues. The accompaniments were played with a knife or bottleneck, and there was the forceful rhythm of the lower strings and the thin whine on the upper strings to reinforce the rough vocal shout. Although he was an exciting religious singer, he will be always thought of as a blues singer because he sang the gospel material in generally conventional texts, but in his blues he was intensely individualistic.

Charley's life didn't change much when the Paramount sessions ended. He had to sing almost every night to make a living, and he moved from small town to small town in the delta. He went back to Lula after the July, 1930, session, and began living a tempestuous life in a plantation cabin with Bertha Lee. He was in his forties and she was sixteen when they began living together. He even mentioned her in one of his songs, "Poor Me."

> "Don't the moon look pretty shining down through the trees,
> I can see Bertha Lee, Lord, but she can't see me ...

They lived in Lula for a year or so, then moved to Holly Springs, in northern Mississippi, about forty miles south-east of Memphis. The store keepers near the cabin where Charley and Bertha Lee lived remembered - talking to Wardlow and Klatzko - that she was "young and wild," that Charley was drinking a lot, and that he and Bertha Lee "... did their share of fighting with each other." Bertha also sang the blues, although she learned nearly all of her songs from Charley. "I couldn't compose things the way he could." Sometimes they sang in the back of the store and one of the owners, a white man named John Allen, played the fiddle with them. It was a rough life. As Bertha Lee remembered, "We broke down many a plantation house having parties every night." For Charley, who did most of the singing, the life was hard and demanding. Bertha Lee was young and strong, but Charley's early years of field work and the constant playing had begun to wear on him. He was already suffering from a heart leakage, so he wasn't able to do any work in the fields and he had to keep singing. They traveled together on most of his trips, and in Cleveland, Mississippi, she remembers sitting and listening while Charley tried to teach his style to a young singer named Chester Burnett, who was to become known in Chicago as "Howling Wolf." "Charley worried with him all day before that man would leave him alone." The limits of Charley's world had again become the vague, violet gray line of the horizon, the meandering dirt tracks across the fields, and the straggling pine woods of the delta. His recordings for Paramount, however, were a tenuous cord that still tied him to the commercial music world. Late in the fall of 1933 he was contacted by Mr. Callaway, the recording director for Vocalion Records, and he and Bertha Lee went together to New York to record in January of 1934.

> *Mr. Callaway sent for us to come up on the train and we were there about three weeks making records. We didn't work all the time, because it took the morning before Charley had his voice ready. The company picked us up at two in the evening and we always did our singing then. There were great big bottles of whiskey sitting on the floor, but I just drank a little to keep my nerve up. I'm not an extreme drinker. Then after we'd finish we had dances for Mr. Callaway and them every evening in the studio...*

They were in the studio three afternoons, Tuesday, Wednesday, and Thursday, January 30, 31, and February 1, 1934, and they went back to Holly Springs a few days later.

It had been four years since Patton had recorded, but there was very little stylistic difference between the later sessions for Vocalion, and the earlier sessions for Paramount. There were differences, but they were more of a technical nature than musical. Vocalion used a much better microphone and positioned it closer to him, so the sound was a little lighter and clearer. Also, he was using a different guitar, and it had a slightly wirier sound. He did two of his earlier songs in different versions. ''Pony Blues'' on Paramount, became ''Stone Pony Blues'' on Vocalion, and ''Tom Rushen Blues'' became ''High Sheriff Blues.'' The singing had changed so little that the difference between the two versions was probably no greater than the difference in the sound of Charley's voice when he'd just started singing at a dance and when he finally finished five or six hours later. The improved recording technique made it obvious that he was having some trouble with hoarseness, but this had always been a problem. He forced his voice, and the strain was evident in all of his sessions. If there was the beginning of a change in his style it was in the guitar accompaniments. In 1934 there was a rhythmic diffuseness, and less of the finger picking that had characterized the accompaniments of 1929 and 1930.

Less than half of the songs that he and Bertha Lee did for Vocalion were issued in the bleak years of the Depression, but even without them he was still a prolific singer by the standards of the early blues period. Nearly sixty titles were released, more than thirty of them blues and the rest gospel and folk songs. In his recordings, more than in the recordings of any other delta singer of the period, it was possible to sense some of the variety of delta music. There were strains from older work songs in pieces like ''When Your Way Gets Dark'' and there were vivid sketches of delta life in blues like ''High Water Everywhere.'' There were dance pieces, country ballads, even bits of white sentimental country music in pieces like ''Some These Days I'll Be Gone.'' In all of the songs his style was the same, a harsh, heavy voice used without embellishment, the melodies emphasizing a few notes within an octave range, the guitar accompaniment roughly following the voice in the upper strings and reiterating the rhythm in the lower strings. In all of them there was, as well, a fierce, almost raging power, and an insistent strength and rhythm.

Perhaps because his music was so much part of the delta soil the young men like Robert Johnson who hung around the dances where he was playing didn't learn much of his style. Patton in many ways came at the end of a period of musical development, and even though he extended and developed the music of the plantations and the cabin rows he still kept its entanglement with the life of the delta counties. The younger men were more restless, they traveled further, and their blues, through the influence of phonograph records, had more than a delta accent. The singing of Charley's close friends, Henry Sims and Willie Brown, and Bertha Lee, was strongly influenced by him, but when Booker White said that he "... wanted to be like old Charley Patton", he meant that he wanted to be like the man Charley Patton more than that he wanted to sing like him. In all of Booker's recorded blues the only suggestion of Patton's style is in the dark voice, and perhaps in the melodic line of "Fixin' To Die," which seems to have some relationship to Charley's beginning vocal phrases in "Frankie And Albert." Son House was already singing when he met Patton, and the only suggestion, again, is in the voice and perhaps in some of his guitar style. Robert Johnson hung around Charley and Son at dances, but it was Son that drew him more than Charley. The only element of Charley's style that he took seems to have been the haunting knife passages on the upper strings in Charley's "When Your Way Gets Dark." They became part of Johnson's later "Come On In My Kitchen." Howling Wolf, perhaps, learned the most from Patton, and despite the changes in his music as the blues moved from the country cabins to the city slums, some of Charley's voice and inflections still color Wolf's style. But if Charley was not to be a strong influence on the development of the blues in the 1930's, he was one of the greatest singers the blues had yet produced, and it is difficult to find another Mississippi singer whose achievement, in breath, range, and consistency, can be measured against his.

Charley and Bertha Lee went back to their cabin when the sessions in New York ended. It was a small, run-down shack at a place called Longswitch, just outside of Holly Grove. It was one of a row of shacks owned by a man named Tom Robinson. Willie and Son had gone up to Lake Cormorant, a small town in De Soto County about twenty five miles south of Memphis, and they heard from Charley a few days after he'd gotten back. Son remembers that it was for some more recordings.[7]

... He got in touch with another record company -- one in Jackson, Mississippi -- called Spear's Phonograph Company, 111 North Farrow Street. This man wanted Charlie to get Willie and I to come down to Jackson to make some church songs. So Charlie sent his wife, Bertha, up after us in a car. We hung around Holly Ridge two or three days before we lit out for Jackson, and we made the songs. This guy wanted us to make like we were "sanctified" people and make some "sanctified" songs and not use our names. So we made a song for him,

"I Had A Dream Last Night Troubled Me," concerning King Nebuchadnezzar. After that, we went on back to Charlie's and we stayed about three more weeks. We went all around through the country playing, all three of us together. So Willie and I went on back to Lake Commorant, where we were living then, and about two weeks after we got back, we got a telegram from Bertha, that was the girl said to be his wife. The telegram said that Charlie was dead...

Bertha Lee lives in Chicago now, a large, good-natured woman who spends her days working in a shabby used clothing store on Chicago's west side. There is a bare bulb hanging from the ceiling, an oil stove in the middle of the floor. Bertha Lee sits at a small table near the door, the radio turned on to a local music station, helping the people who lean against the heaped piles of old clothes trying to decide if something will fit. "That's too small for you, dear, there's another skirt down in the pile somewhere that's more your size." She has glasses now, and usually wears a dark dress and a sweater as she sits at her table. She remarried after Charley died, and she was widowed again when her second husband died a few years ago, but she has lived in Chicago since 1949 and she has friends and family to keep the evenings from getting too lonely. More than thirty years have passed since she was the "young and wild" girl who lived with Charley Patton in a shack in the Mississippi delta, but she still smiles when she thinks back to the singing and the dances, and even to the fights that she and Charley had while they lived together. He died only a few weeks after they got back from New York. Like most men who become local heroes there were stories that he had been poisoned, or that he had died of a tetanus infection from a knife wound, or that he had been killed in a fight, but his heart, already damaged, had been weakened by chronic bronchitis, and the life he was leading was too chaotic for him to rest. Bertha Lee looked out through the window, across the street to a crowd of children playing on the sidewalk, their scarves wrapped around their necks against the winter cold and their ears covered with bright cloth ear muffs.

Charley was playing for a white dance - you have to work so much harder at a white dance in the South, they don't want to stop dancing. When he come home he was so hoarse he couldn't talk and he couldn't get his breath. He had to get up out of bed at night and open the windows so he could get some air. He lived three weeks after that but he was too weak to do anything. He was laying across my lap when he died.

3. SON HOUSE

A tall, gangling man, moving a little stiffly from his long years as a field hand and a laborer. At the edge of a crowd his white Stetson hat turning like a leaf in the spring wind as he answers questions in a low voice. His face - still thin and handsome despite the lines etched by the worries and the disappointments of his sixty-three years - looks from one to another of the young white faces pressed around him, unsure of their attitudes toward him, unsure of their response to his music. A delta blues man, the only singer left of the group around Charley Patton, Eddie James House Jr., "Son" House, at a folk festival in New York City in the late spring of 1965.

Until the summer of 1964 the delta blues was still only a few names on phonograph records. The field song elements in the music, the glimpsed presence of endless work, drinking, prison, the sexuality of the words, the raw strength of the singing - from these sources it wasn't difficult to relate the delta style to the life of the sharecroppers and field hands living in the steaming swelter of the Yazoo cotton country. But art is only in part sociology. Each of the delta singers came from the same backgrounds, from the same rows of plantation shacks, the same weathered clusters of buildings around a crossroads country store, but each of them sang in his own style. Until the 1963 trip by Wardlow and Klatzko there were only a few scattered reminiscences of the delta singers. "Robert Johnson played one night with us at a dance hall in West Memphis." "Charley Patton was a large, fat man who come 'round the cabin when my daddy was living." "Son House was playing in a road house with Charley Patton when I seen him. He got drunk and climbed up on a table to give a sermon." Not enough to fill in the human quality of the individual singers. Without the background of their lives it was impossible to tell why their voices were different, their emotional concerns were different, and their music - even though it came from the same sources and backgrounds - was different. It has only been since the early weeks of July, 1964, that it has been possible to discuss the

57

delta blues as personal art instead of impersonal sociology. Working separately, but within a few days of each other, John Fahey, Bill Barth, and Henry Vestine, driving from California, found Skip James in the Tunica County Hospital; and Dick Waterman, Phil Spiro, and Nick Perls, driving down from Cambridge and New York, found Son House. When they located him it was another long drive - Son had left Mississippi and moved to Rochester, New York, twenty years before - but their long drive has meant not only priceless information about the great Mississippi singers, but also the return to music of one of the greatest of these blues men, still singing in the purest delta blues strain. Through Son, and through Bertha Lee Patton, who had finally been traced to Chicago by Bernard Klatzko a few months before Son was located, the story of the Mississippi blues has become a living, human story.

In the winter of 1965 Son talked about his life to Julius Lester, a young writer living in New York, and his reminiscences not only filled in the backgrounds of his own musical style, but also of the music of the other singers he encountered in his wanderings. He was born on March 21, 1902, on a farm in Coahoma County, just outside of Lyon, a small town a few miles from Clarksdale. As he told Lester,[1.]

> *... They called it Riverton, and right down the road a little past Riverton -- about two miles -- is where I was born. After I got up around seven or eight years old, my mother took me to Louisiana, and that's mostly where I grew up to call myself a man. We moved to a place called Tallulah, Louisiana. That's up in the north part of Louisiana, across the river from Vicksburg.*

> *My mother and my father they separated, and when I got up to be some size, I started working. One while, I was gathering moss down in Algiers, Louisiana. That was in 1917, '17, and on up to about '20. I wasn't big enough to occupy a heavy job. I was gathering that grey moss out of trees. Did it near about like they do cotton. Bale it up and ship it away and they would make mattresses and things out of it. I was quite young then -- twenty, twenty-one -- along in that category.*

> *I wasn't playing guitar then. I was mostly a church man. Brought up in church and didn't believe in anything else but church, and it always made me mad to see a man with a guitar and singing these blues and things. Just wasn't brought up to it. Brought up to sing in choirs. That's all I believed in, then.*

> *My father, though, was kind of ratty along then. He had seven brothers and they had a little band that played music all the time for the Saturday night balls. He played a bass horn. He had been a church man, but he had gotten out. Finally, he*

went back to church and laid it all down, quit drinking, and became a deacon. He went pretty straight from then on.

After my mother died, I left and came back up in Mississippi where the rest of my people was. So I was just to and fro then. I wouldn't stay anywhere too long after I got to be called myself a man, you know. I just wanted to ramble. I wouldn't get too far away from home, though. I'd get up around Memphis, over in Arkansas, back through Louisiana, and on back to Mississippi. And I'd make a living by working in the cotton fields. I could plow, pick, and chop cotton. One while, I worked for a man who was in the cattle business. That was down in Louisiana and that was when I started wearing a cowboy hat. I got that style from the other guys. The hat I wore was a big brown with a white band around the crown, and when I went to playing guitar, I was still wearing it. I liked it. But something happened and I got rid of it. It got too old or something, so by the time I was making records, I wasn't wearing it.

At that time, there was mostly farm work, and sometimes it got pretty critical. Low wages and -- well, people kind of suffered a little during some of those years. Suffered right smart. In some places, they got along a little better than they did in others. But they stayed up against it mostly. Bad housing and all that kind of stuff. Of course, they'd get plenty of just old common food, but they didn't make enough money to do any good. Some of those that grew crops -- if they paid their debts for the food they ate during the year, why, if they came out and cleared as much as forty or fifty dollars for a year, they were satisfied. Out of a whole year's work! Of course, along then, they didn't see into it too much because they'd been used to it for so long. They didn't worry over it because they always knew if they didn't have the money, they was still going to eat and have a place to stay, such as it was. So they didn't complain and worry too much about it.

After they commenced waking up, some started going different places and came back with the news that they were doing so much better. "Up in such-and-such-a-place, they pay so-much-and-so-much. That's what I make." Well, that wakes the other guys up. He sees his old buddy all dressed up and looking so nice, and so they comment from one to another and commence to easing out to these different places. If they get far as St. Louis, oh, Jesus! They thought they was way somewhere.

I did it myself! I had a friend who was up there working in the Commonwealth Steel Plant in St. Louis. He came back and was telling me about it, and the first thing you know, I'd

59

sneaked out and gone to St. Louis. We were getting a dollar an hour along then. That was big money, you know. That was way back yonder. A dollar an hour! Whooo! That was along in 1922 or '23. The Commonwealth Steel Plant. We lived in St. Louis, and the plant was in East St. Louis, just across the river. Making that dollar an hour. I was a big shot then. I stayed up there about six or eight months and got the hot-foot again and came on back down in Mississippi. I wasn't contented anywhere long. I was young and just loved to ramble.

I was just ramblified, you know. Especially after I started playing music. That was the one thing gave it to me. People wanting us to come over in Arkansas to play for picnics, and we just didn't want to be stationary, to be obligated to anybody. We figured we could make it better without plowing so much.

I started playing guitar in 1928, but I got the idea around about 1927. I saw a guy named Willie Wilson and another one named Reuben Lacy. All before then, I just hated to see a guy with a guitar. I was so churchy! I came along to a little place they call Matson, a little below Clarksdale. It was on a Saturday and these guys were sitting out front of a place and they were playing. Well, I stopped, because the people were all crowded around. This boy, Willie Wilson, had a thing on his finger like a small medicine bottle, and he was zinging it, you know. I said, "Jesus! Wonder what's that he's playing?" I knew that guitars hadn't usually been sounding like that. So I eases up close enough to look and I see what he has on his finger. "Sounds good!" I said. "Jesus! I like that!" And from there, I got the idea and said, "I believe I want to play one of them things." So I bought an old piece of guitar from a fella named Frank Hopkins. I gave him a dollar-and-a-half for it. It was nearly all to pieces, but I didn't know the difference. The back was all broken in, but I got it from him and began to try to play. It didn't have but five strings on it, though. So I showed it to Willie Wilson and explained to him what I wanted to do. I wanted to learn to play. He said, "Well, you'll never learn this way. You need another string. Takes six strings. It's all busted in the back, too. Tell you what I'll do. I'll see if I can fix it up for you." So he got some tape and stuff and taped it all up and got a string and put that on and then he tuned it. He tuned it in Spanish to make it easier for me to start. Then he showed me a couple of chords. I got me an old bottle. Cut my finger a couple of times trying to fix the thing like his, but finally I started to zinging, too. Finally, I got the idea about how to tune it myself. I used to be a leader in the choir and they were singing the old vocal music at that time, you know, like the "do-re-mi's", so I got the idea to make the guitar go like that, and in a couple of weeks time, I was able to play a little tune. It was a little

tune I'd heard Willie Wilson play called, "Hold Up, Sally,
Take Your Big Legs Offa Mine." So the next time he came by,
I showed him I could play it. He said, "Come on and play with
me tonight." It was Saturday night. I said, "I ain't good
enough for that." He said, "Oh, yes, you is. You just play
that. I'll back you up." So I started with him just like that.
Finally, he left from around there, but I kept on playing and
got better and better, you know. I'd set up and concentrate on
songs, and then went to concentrating on me rhyming words,
rhyming my own words. "I can make my own songs," I said.
And that's the way I started.

Many of the delta men went into recording studios during this period,
but Willie Wilson does not seem to have done any recording. Lacy
recorded for Paramount a year after Son heard him play. It was only two
years before Son himself recorded for Paramount. He went to Lula to
see his aunt, met Charley Patton while he was there, and through Charley
he did a test for H.C. Spears in Jackson. In his conversation with Lester
he remembered,[2.]

There was this man, A. C. Laibley, who was Charlie's manager
at that time. He was in Grafton, Wisconsin. That's where the
Paramount Record laboratory was. He came down on a little
tour hunting talent, and he stopped by and told Charlie they
wanted him to come up for recordings again. Well, Charlie
had been recording for them and he told them about me. So
they said, "Bring him along with you and bring Willie Brown."
So he left a hundred dollars for expenses. He got another fella
that had a car. This other fella had a group, a gospel group,
and they called themselves the Delta Big Four. They made
themselves famous with a song called "Four and Twenty Elders
On Their Knees". His name was Will Ford and he had a good
car, so A. C. Laibley left the money for him to drive us up
there. There was a girl named Louise Johnson who came
along with us. She and Willie were both from Robinsonville.
So we went up there and made our recordings separately,
except for about two songs Willie and I played together. I
recorded "Preachin' Blues", "Black Mama", "Mississippi
County Farm", and "Clarksdale Moan". Willie Brown and I
played that last one together. I think that's about all. Close
as I can get to it. It's been so long.

The girl playing the piano, Louise, well, we'd spike in and
help her a little bit. She was a good piano player, but being up
there and being among a lot of people, well, you know, some
people get nervous. So we'd cheer her up by yelling to her and
saying funny things and we'd hit a lick or two with the guitars.
Just to give her more spirit.

I got paid forty dollars for making those records. At that time, I just had the big eyes. Forty dollars! Making it that easy and that quick! It'd take me near about a whole year to make forty dollars in the cotton patch. I was perfectly satisfied. I showed off a whole lot with that when I got back to Lula, Mississippi.

The sessions were held in Grafton, Wisconsin, sometime in the summer of 1930, and Son did three long blues and three shorter ones. Copies have not yet been located of all of the songs, but the three long pieces have been found: "My Black Mama, Parts 1 and 2" on Paramount 13042, "Preachin' The Blues, Parts 1 and 2" on Paramount 13013, and "Dry Spell Blues, Parts 1 and 2" on Paramount 12990. Each of the three was among the greatest blues performances recorded in the 'twenties. "Dry Spell Blues" was the most socially directed of the three, and it had some of the largeness of concept of Patton's "High Water Everywhere."

Them dry spell blues are fallin', drivin' people from door to door.
Dry spell blues are fallin', drivin' people from door to door.
Them dry spell blues has put everybody on the kindlin' floor.

Now the people down South soon won't have no homes.
Lord, the people down South soon won't have no homes.
Lord, this dry spell have parched all the cotton and corn ....

Pork chops forty-five cents a pound, cotton is only ten.
Pork chops forty-five cents a pound, cotton is only ten.
I can't keep no women, no no now or then.

So dry old boweevil turn up its nose and die.
So dry old boweevil turn up its nose and die.
Now ain't nothing to do to make moonshine and rye ....

It's a dry old spell everywhere I been.
Oh it's a dry old spell everywhere I been.
I believe to my soul this old world is bound to end.

Lord, I stood in my back yard, wrung my hands and grieved.
I stood in my back yard, I wrung my hands and grieved.
Oh I couldn't see nothing, couldn't see nothing green.

Oh Lord, have mercy if you please.
Oh Lord, have mercy if you please.
Make your rain come down and give our poor hearts ease ....

In the other blues there was less of Patton's concern with place, and the pieces had a highly individualistic textual and musical orientation. There was little use of the unison melody in his accompaniments;

usually the guitar played a bare, drumming rhythm in the lower strings and Son sang against it with considerable melodic freedom. His voice was strident and tense, and the rhythms had little of Patton's regularity. There was also much more vocal embellishment, and the guitar, played with a bottleneck, developed its own set figures at the end of each vocal phrase. There was no harmonic change in the accompaniment of "Preachin' The Blues," and the harmonic progression in "My Black Mama" was limited to the bass note played with the thumb. "My Black Mama" was a loosely grouped set of verses more or less well known through the delta, but in "Preachin' The Blues," even though many of the verses were also conventional, it was possible to sense some of the confusion in Son that gave his music its decisiveness. He had been unable to decide completely between the irreligious life of the blues man and the Christian life of the preacher. It is an indecision that still disturbs him more than thirty years later. As he sang in the blues, "I have religion on this very day ... But the womens and whiskey, well, they would not let me pray." He feels that "Preachin' The Blues" itself is a reflection of his confusion. "I can't hold God in one hand and the Devil in the other one ..."

Oh, I'm gonna get me a religion, I'm gonna join the Baptist church.
Oh, I'm gonna get me a religion, I'm gonna join the Baptist church.
I'm gonna be a Baptist preacher, and I sure won't have to work.

Oh, I'm preach these blues and I want everybody to shout.
Umh, I want everybody to shout.
I'm gonna do like a prisoner, I'm gonna roll my time on out.

Oh, 'way in my room I bow down to pray.
Oh, in my room I bow down to pray.
Well, the blues came 'long and they blown my (babe) away.

Oh, I wish I had me a heaven of my own.
  Sp. (Great God Almighty!)
Umh, heaven of my own.
Well, I'd give all my women a long, long happy home.

Well, I love my baby just like I love myself.
Umh, just like I love myself.
Well, if she don't have me she won't have nobody else.

Well, I'm a poor man, I'm gonna kneel down in prayer.
Oh, I'm a poor man, gonna kneel down in prayer.
Well, I guess I'm gonna do my preachin' (   )

Now, I met the blues this morning walking just like a man.
Umh, walking just like a man.
I said "Good morning, blues, now gimme your right hand."

63

Now, there's nothing now baby, lord, that's gonna worry my mind.
Umh, now that's gonna worry my mind.
Oh, to satisfy, I got the longest line.

Oh, I got to stay on the job, I ain't got no time to lose.
Umh, I ain't got no time to lose.
I swear to God, I got to preach these gospel blues.
   sp. (Great God Almighty!)

Oh, I'm gonna preach these blues until my feet have set down.
Oh, I'm gonna preach these blues now, until my feet have set down.
Well, it's very (constructive) I want you to jump straight up and
    down.

In the straining impatience of the melody there was still some of the
exhortation from his years as a rural preacher, and he was forced into
considerable rhythmic irregularity by the emotionalism of his singing.
The accompaniment was an insistent 8/8 pattern that continued without
change through the piece.

Example 10
(Preaching Blues)

His "My Black Mama" was almost as irregular in the singing, but the lines were built around the hesitation in the opening phrase that was characteristic of the axe songs. In these songs the singer usually hesitates on the first beat of the measure as the blade of the axe bites into the log, and Son kept this hesitation in most of the verses; even though it meant breaking the line into two separate rhythmic units to give himself room for the hesitation. The accompaniment was in a mixed rhythm that had strong ties to the African background rhythms. The harmony was the root chord of I, V, I, IV, I, and the rhythmic pattern was,

4/4, 4/4, 4/4, 4/4, 6/4, 4/4, 4/4, 6/4, 4/4, 4/4

In an unguarded moment Son reiterated his feeling that he should never have left the church in an introduction to "Preachin' The Blues" at a concert at the University of Indiana in November, 1964.[3.]

This is one on me. Just (as) well admit it. This is the truth. 'Cause, some of it is a little addition, but the biggest of it is the truth. I used to be a preacher. I was brought up in church and I started preaching before I started this junk. Well, I got in a little bad company one time and they said, "Aw, c'mon, take a little nip with us. "I says, "Naw." "Aw, c'mon!" So I took a little nip. None of the members were around, so I took the little nip. And that one little nip called for another big nip. So there got to be a rumor around among my members, you know. And I began to wonder, now how can I stand up in the pulpit and preach to them, tell them how to live, and quick as I dismiss the congregation and I see ain't nobody looking and I'm doing the same thing. I says, that's not right. But I kept nipping around there and it got to be a public thing. I says, well, I got to do something, 'cause I can't hold God in one hand and the Devil in the other one. Them two guys don't get along together too well. I got to turn one of 'em loose. So I got out of the pulpit. So I said the next time I make a record, I'm gon' to name it "Preachin Blues." I'm preaching on this side and the blues on that side. I says, well, I'll just put 'em together and name it "Preachin Blues."

It is this indecision which seems to give his blues some of their intensity of emotion, some of their pain and anguish. Often the most moving piece that he sings in a set is a religious song like "Motherless Children Have A Hard Time," the guitar playing a unison line with the bottleneck behind the voice. For Son singing the blues means a choice, and he still seems unable to reconcile himself to the choice he has made. Sometimes in a club he introduces each song with the same mumbled introduction, saying again and again,

65

> *When they found me they got the news that I was a part-time preacher. Well, I was a preacher for a while, but I got to slipping around and doing ... other things. Then I went back to being a preacher; so you could say I was just a part-time preacher.*

In the early 'forties Son left Mississippi and moved to Rochester. [4.]

> *... A friend of mine had moved up there and was working for a firm they call Simelton and Gold. They were making some kind of war equipment and he wrote and told me about them and what good wages they were paying. So I went on up. I worked on that job for a payday and then I quit. I didn't like it too well. So then I got a job with the New York Central out to East Rochester in the dispatch shop where they make boxcars and things like that. I got a job as a rivet-heater and kept that about two or three years. I got a promotion from the railroad company and they sent me over to Buffalo to get signed up for a job as a porter. There was a big fat colored guy over there doing the hiring at that time, so I got right on and stayed with that job ten, eleven years.*

He kept playing mostly because he was still close to Willie Brown, and they saw each other on occasional trips. Son went back to Mississippi for a vacation, and Willie even came to Rochester for a brief period. With Willie's death about 1948 Son finally put his music aside. "I said, 'Well, sir. All my boys are gone.' That was when I stopped playing."

"After he died, I just decided I wouldn't fool with playing any more. I don't even know what I did with the guitar."

Son looks back over the years without much bitterness, but he feels that all of them should have continued to record through the 'thirties, despite the depression that hung over Mississippi. "We did our best things then, after we'd got a little used to recording and knew what we wanted to do."

Son was able to record again in 1942, when he was still playing regularly, and his individual style had reached a high point of development. He went back to Mississippi for a visit and he was in Robinsonville visiting relatives when Alan Lomax came to a local crossroads store and set up portable recording equipment to collect material for the Library of Congress archives. Son sang for him all day, even showing him tunings and discussing his techniques; then he found that all he was to be paid was a Coca Cola. He still smiles about it. "All I got was a bottle of coke, but it was good and cold." It was ironic for everyone who had been looking for Son for nearly a dozen years to learn that Alan had known of his whereabouts all during this time.

In 1942 Son had lost some of the tense emotionalism of the first sessions, but his style was unchanged. There was still the hesitation before the beginning of the vocal phrase, the barren drumming on the bass strings of the guitar, and the whine of the bottleneck on the upper strings. He had developed the interplay between the voice and guitar to a high level of complexity. The guitar used melodic material that was often closely related to the vocal line, but still free from it, instead of the repetitive patterns in his older recordings. The integration in tone and rhythm between the two voices, the guitar's and his own, was perhaps the most sensitive that any blues singer has ever achieved. In the "Depot Blues," or as it was inadvertently titled for a later release, "I Ain't Gonna Cry No More," the guitar's melodic line moves for some measures in unison with the voice; then it ends the phrase with its own melodic materials, keeping the same hesitation in the first beat of the measure. He played it in the standard guitar tuning, which he calls the "Key of Minor."

Example 11.

Some of his finest blues were recorded on that hot summer afternoon in Robinsonville. He had honed down his old "My Black Mama," giving the verses a greater tension and cohesiveness. The new version, "My Black Woman," was moving and effective blues poetry. The text has been extensively analyzed in the book "The Poetry Of The Blues."

Well, did you get that letter I mailed in your back yard.
Uumm - that I mailed in your back yard.
It's mighty sad to say that your best friend, we have got to part.

Well, I got a letter this morning, how do you reckon it read?
Got a letter this morning, how do you reckon it read?
"Better hurry, hurry, 'cause the gal you love is dead."

You know I got my suitcase and I took on down the road,
Uumm, took on down the road,
But when I got there she was laying on the cooling bo'd.

You know I walked up close and I looked down in her face,
Uumm, I looked down in her face.
You a good old gal, but you got to lay down to judgement day.

You know, I fold my arms and I slowly walk away.
Uumh, I slowly walk away.
You a good old gal, I just can't take your place.

Also in the session he emerged as a songster. Unlike Patton, however, his songs were as much individual compositions as his blues. One of them, a song concerning his feelings at the beginning of the Second World War, was unlike anything recorded by any other blues singer. It was in waltz tempo, but he sang it with the heavy voice and strongly rhythmic guitar of the delta blues style.

No use to shedding no tears, no use to having no fears.
This war may last you for years.

Well, the red white and blues (?) at you,
You ought to do everything that you can.
Buy war saving stamps, young men go to the camps,
Be brave and take this stand.
    No use to shedding no tears, no use to having no fears,
    This war may last you for years.

Oh the struggle sometime will upset your mind;
So you won't know just what to do.
Just keep pushing keep shoving, don't be angry be loving,
Be faithful and honest and true.
    No use to shedding no tears, no use to having no fears,
    This war may last you for years.

You can say yes or no, but we got to win this war;
Because General McArthur's one friend.
There won't be enough japs to shoot a little game of craps;
Because the biggest of the all will be dead.
    No use to shedding no tears, no use to having no fears.
    This war may last you for years.

This war sure do bother our mother and father,
Our sisters and brothers, too.
Dear friends and relations, the war's end creation,
Don't let this worry you.
    No use to shedding no tears, no use to having no fears,
    This war may last you for years.

(This War Will Last You for Years)

This was also accompanied in standard tuning. Most of his bottleneck blues, however, still are done in the "cross Spanish" tuning, e-b-e'-#g-b-e'', and he chords the tonic E on the seventh fret of the first string and the eighth fret of the second string, as in standard tuning. He wears a piece of metal tubing on his third finger, using it on the middle strings as well as the top string for the unison melody. Often he stops the sound of the strings with his second finger to keep the sound from becoming muddied. Nearly all of the right hand picking is done with the first finger plucking the string upward, after a strong down stroke with the thumb on a bass string. There is as much embellishment of tone and pitch in the bottleneck playing as there is in his voice. The interplay between his hands has almost the grace and fluidity of a dance as they move in their endless patterns over the neck of his metal National guitar.

It has been difficult for Son to adjust to playing again, despite the careful attention of Dick Waterman, one of the men who found him and who now travels with him. There is often a sense of isolation about him, as though he still half expects to find Willie Brown or Charley Patton sitting beside him with their guitars. As he has grown older, too, his confusions about his own relationship to the blues have increased; so he is sometimes indecisive as a performer. To hear Son at his best, however, is one of the most moving experiences that the blues can offer. He seems to look uncomfortably out at his audience; then his head goes back and his eyes close, the eyeballs uncomfortably rolling up under his eyelids. He clutches the guitar, and with a nervous gesture hits the string with the metal slide. In the whining, trembling sound of the guitar and the almost painful outcry of his voice is the smell of weeds along the Sunflower River, and the sound of the wind in the trees along a red clay road, the stifling heat of the July sun in the endless rows of the cotton fields. Afterwards, outside of the club where he was playing, he tries to answer questions, standing with his guitar propped up on the sidewalk, his jacket carefully buttoned and his tie straightened under his collar. But after a moment the questions usually die away, and he is able to get to the bus that takes him back to Rochester. Son is so completely the embodiment of the delta blues style that it often seems difficult for him to reach across the differences between himself and the people that want to talk to him. His music, however, stretches across the differences, and in a room as he sings, the whole world of the Mississippi delta seems to crowd within the walls.

4. SKIP JAMES

Each of the delta blues men has had to find his own resolution between the fiery Christianity of southern Baptist or Methodist churches and the amorality of his music. Some, like Patton, were able to move from one kind of song to the other, almost unconcerned with the conflict between the two attitudes. Others, like Son House, hesitate, irresolute and uneasy. One of the most consciously creative singers of the delta, Skip James, has given most of his life to the church, but his blues still reflect some of the introspective brooding that went into his decision.

Like Patton, Skip was born into a religious family, but his father was more active in the church than Patton's. When Skip was born - June 9, 1902 on the Whitehead Plantation a mile and a half from Bentonia, in Yazoo County north of Jackson - his father was preaching to a Baptist congregation on the plantation. His parents, Reverend Nehemiah James and Phyllis James, named him after his father. His given name was Nehemiah - but Skip has said, ''In my young days I used to like dancing and I'd skip around at the parties people used to have in their houses so they give me the name of Skippy.'' The Skippy became Skip when he was a young man. He was an only child, and he grew up wandering alone on the banks of the Big Black River, just behind the plantation. He began to learn the piano and organ as a boy, and he played for services in his father's church. He was able to get to school, unlike most of the other delta singers, and he finished high school in Yazoo City. He began playing the guitar about the same time, learning some chords and changes from two musicians at Bentonia, Rich Griffin and Henry Stuckee. Stuckee played with a simple two-finger picking and Griffin ''wrapped behind a fiddle,'' straight rhythm with an accented second and fourth beat of the measure. They played country ''frolics,'' and from them Skip ''...got an idea about music.'' He learned some of the tunes they did together and recorded one of them, ''Drunken Spree,'' years later on a recording, Paramount 13111, that was listed in a Paramount release

71

sheet but has still not been found. Skip's guitar style is a complex and distinctly original three-finger picking technique, but he learned the roots of his music on the plantation where he lived as a boy.

Because of his close relationship with his mother and father Skip never left the South, but he was restless as a young man, and he spent most of his life moving from one part of the South to another. With his high school education he could have gone into teaching, but instead he spent years drifting as laborer, as though he wasn't entirely at ease either singing in road houses and dance halls or following in his father's footsteps into the church. When he finished school he left Mississippi and went across the river into Arkansas. He worked in a saw mill in Weona and met a pianist named Will Crabtree, who was working in a saloon on Market Street in Marked Tree, Arkansas, a town a few miles from Weona on U. S. 63 north of Memphis. From Will he learned enough of the blues to begin developing his own style as a blues pianist, and when he went back to Mississippi he worked as a musician for fifty cents or a dollar a night, playing either piano or guitar. He was in Memphis in 1926 or 1927 and heard Bessie Smith and Clarence Williams, who were touring with a stage show. He played some country dances around the delta, but he was afraid to play on the rougher plantations. "I'd take a chance some time, but in those plantations they had those rusty old pistols..." He met another pianist, Little Brother Montgomery, in Yazoo City, and they went into Vicksburg together. He learned his "Special Rider Blues" from Little Brother, and Montgomery learned his famous "Vicksburg Blues" from Skip.

Skip remembers learning his first blues, "Alabama Blues," on the Bentonia plantation when he was about twelve years old; so he had been playing for nearly fifteen years when Paramount Records began to take an interest in the delta singers. He learned the song with the old "straight wrap" accompaniment, "frailing," as he calls it, and he still plays it that way fifty years later. During one of his stays in Jackson the Paramount scout H. C. Spears got in touch with him. "I'd like you to come down tomorrow and play a piece or two." Skip remembers that there were forty or fifty singers at Spears' music store when he got there the next day, but he was the only one that "passed." He sang two verses of "Devil Got My Woman" for Spears and Spears told him that was enough. Spears signed him to a two year contract with Paramount, and in the early spring of 1931 sent him on the bus to Arthur Laiblee at the Paramount studios in Grafton, Wisconsin. He remembers doing twenty-six titles over three days of recording. Most of them were delta pieces, but others were composed during the sessions. As he says, "I could compose a song in three minutes." On the last afternoon Laiblee mentioned the popularity of the "Forty-Four Blues" and asked Skip, "Could you make a record comparing to that?" They talked about the caliber of the revolver and Skip decided on something smaller, a 22-20. "Do you think you could make a record on that? You only have three minutes." Skip had his song within the three minutes and recorded it with piano accompaniment. The words were undistinguished, but his piano solo in the middle of the record was a hard-rubbed gem of country blues playing.

Example 12.

He went back to Mississippi when the sessions were finished and moved in with a young singer named Johnny Temple, who was living in Jackson. He waited for months for his records to bring him some kind of recognition, but he still angrily remembers that he was never fully paid for the recording and that the company went out of business before his records were even distributed. Disappointed, and unable to find much work in the depression panic that had seized Mississippi, he suddenly decided to join his father in Dallas. He began working in the church in Texas in 1932, and it was thirty-two years before he sang the blues again.

In his brief working sessions in Grafton Skip had already left a major group of blues on record, and he has added to this body of work since he again became part of the blues world in 1964. His style was one of the most distinctive to come out of the delta, and it was dominated by an intense lyricism that shaped every element of the music. His singing was closely related to the field holler, and he was freer in his vocal rhythms than men like Patton or Son House. In his accompaniment there was often a complex picking style in the upper strings, with a bass pattern that had the sombre inevitability of the movement of the sun across the Mississippi sky.

The rhythmic subtlety was one of his most distinctive characteristics, but he was also one of the few singers to use a falsetto voice, instead of the heavier Mississippi vocal tone, and he used melodies and harmonies that were more definitely minor than those in the blues of other singers. He used two tunings for most of the songs with guitar accompaniment, the standard e-a-d-g-b-e', and what he called "cross note," e-b-e-g-b-e''. He thinks of it as "cross note" because "... the major and minor cross during the music." Played open the strings would be an E minor chord, but for the tonic position he generally holds his first finger on the first fret of the g string, raising it to the major third, g#. One of the sounds that typifies his accompaniment style is his tonic grouping over the low e fundamental. He plays the open e string with his thumb; then descends on the upper first and third strings, the e'' and g, from the seventh to the fifth to the third fret; then to the open top strings, holding the g# in the third string. The fingering inverts the usual descending thirds of this harmonic pattern, and they become the more interesting interval of the major sixth. He usually played a melodic line in unison with the voice, like most of the other Mississippi singers, but he filled the openings between the vocal phrases with rhythmic figures in the guitar that had a distinct complexity.

In their melodic and rhythmic outlines his blues were deceptively simple. The beat had an almost monotonous regularity and the melodies moved in easy intervalic relationships. But by limiting himself in these areas he could move with less restraint in others. There were display pieces like the hymn "I'm So Glad," with its mixing of falsetto and natural voice and its brilliantly difficult accompaniment; but even in a less obvious piece, like "Special Rider Blues," he made considerable use of complex details like triplets, half measures, and suspensions in the accompaniment, and mordents, the falsetto, and cadential embellishment in his voice.

Example 13

The triplets in the opening measures were probably derived from his piano style. This was a standard early blues piano technique, and he made extensive use of it in his own playing. The mordent came each time on the third of the scale, the turn ending on a definite minor modality. With the mordent on the third he had considerable ambiguity in the major-minor elements of the piece. The scale was a gapped pentatonic, with the second and fourth present only as passing tones. He generally used the pentatonic or hexatonic blues scales, even in the pieces with piano accompaniment. In the piano pieces the fourth became a scale tone, and the harmonic movement from I to IV was more clearly defined than in his guitar pieces.

Example 14

(If you haven't any hay)

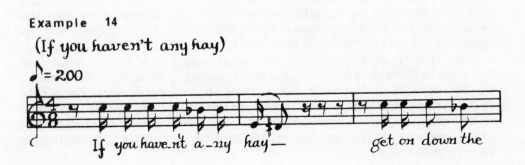

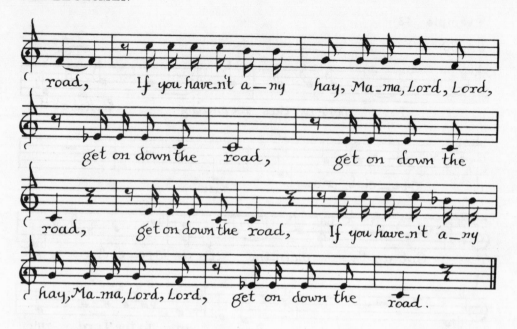

The e is an altered mordent in the voice, but in the accompaniment it is played as the minor e flat. His use of the mordent on the third was consistent in his blues pieces and had the subtlety - in the equivocation between major and minor - of the less restricted field holler. The piano style itself is as complex in its irregularity as his guitar style is subtle in its restraint. He bends over the keys, his left hand tentatively drumming on an open chord as he finishes a vocal phrase; then the right hand suddenly moves into a hurried run or a crashing chord rhythm. There has never been anything in music that even vaguely resembles Skip's piano style. At moments in the first recordings there was an almost frenzied incoherence as his fingers groped to find a rhythmic figure that was beyond the limits of the blues idiom. His foot could be heard urgently tapping an irregular rhythm, against which his voice and the piano surged in swirls of sound. His playing, now, has lost some of its fire, but the four pieces he did with piano accompaniment in February, 1931, "Little Cow And Calf Is Gonna Die Blues," "How Long 'Buck'", "22-20 Blues," "If You Haven't Any Hay Get On Down The Road," will always stand uniquely alone in the history of the blues.

Although Skip was a skilled blues poet his verse material never had the vividness and the individuality of his music. Sometimes the blues was begun with a strong emotional motivation, but he usually drew on conventional material for the rest of the verses. One afternoon he was cutting timber at Cypress Grove, about nine miles from Bentonia on the road to Flora, and it was "...hot and contrary" working in the swamp; so he decided to write a song about it, using the same idea as the religious song, "I don't care where they bury my body; just so my soul's in heaven." But his "CypressGrove Blues" became only an erotic complaint, and even in the opening verse there was no effort to describe his afternoon in the swamp.

> I would rather be buried in some Cypress Grove,
> I would rather be buried in some Cypress Grove,
> I'm going away now, I'm going away to stay.
>
> Lord, I'm going away now, I'm going away to stay.
> Lord, I'm going away now, I'm going away to stay.
> Be all right, pretty mama, might need my help some day...

Except for his religious pieces, the verses were usually erotic, and they were almost always derivative. He was able to suggest a larger social context in some of his verses, however, most obviously in his ''Hard Time Killin' Floor Blues,'' one of the few open social statements to come out of the delta.

> Hard times here 'no; everywhere you go.
> Times is harder than ever been before.
>
> And the people are drifting from door to door,
> Can't find no heaven I don't care where they go.
> Umum ...
>
> Let me tell you people just before I go,
> These hard times 'll kill you (just try long so)
> Umum ...
>
> When you hear me singing my old lonesome song
> These hard times can last us so very long.
> Umum ...
>
> If I ever get off this chittlin' floor
> I'll never get down this road no more.
> Lord, lord, lord, lord,
>   I never get down this road no more.
>
> If you said you had money you better be sure,
> 'Cause these hard times'll drive you from door to door.
> Umum...
>
> Sing this song and I ain't gonna sing no more.
> Sing this song and I ain't gonna sing no more.
> Umum...
>   Hard times'll drive you from door to door.

When he was most individual the pieces were still shaped by the lonely field hollers that dominated his vocal style. In ''Devil Got My Woman,'' one of his most moving blues, there was even the ruminative quality of the holler in the text, as the verse form grew from a simple rhymed couplet to a complex six line verse that ended the song. It had the looseness and the lonely introspection of a man singing softly to his mule, as he plodded behind it in the mud furrow of a spring field.

I'd rather be the devil than be that woman's man.
I'd rather be the devil than be that woman's man.

Oh, nothing but the devil changed my baby's mind.
Oh, nothing but the devil changed my baby's mind.

Oh, laid down last night,
Laid down last night,
Laid down last night,
Start to take my rest.
Oh, my mind got to rambling like the wild geese from the west.

Oh, woman I love,
    Woman that I love,
    Woman I love,
Stoled her from my best friend.
But he got lucky, stoled her back again.
And he got lucky, stoled her back again.

A musician like Skip, considering himself part of the commercial music business, probably would have changed his style considerably if he had continued playing during the 1930's and the 1940's, just as most of the other young singers of the 1920's did. He was competitive as well as musically sophisticated enough to have moved into a number of musical areas, perhaps even into jazz piano. But his decision to join the church meant, instead, that he stopped playing secular music, and when he was found in Mississippi in the summer of 1964, his old style was still in his fingers and his voice.

Skip's restless wandering went on for more than twenty years, despite his decision to work in the church. He had been to Texas with his father when he was still in his teens, and in 1932 he moved to Dallas to help his father organize a gospel quartet. After a year of traveling to churches in Texas, Oklahoma, and Arkansas his father was offered a position as head of a Baptist seminary in Birmington. Skip returned with him and studied for the ministry; then he went back to his traveling, this time as a minister with a gospel group that did the singing. He gave services as a visiting preacher, a widespread practice in southern Baptist churches. He gave a twenty to thirty minute "sermonette," with music to introduce and close the service. He toured through Mississippi, Alabama, Oklahoma, even parts of Kansas. He was still unsure of his calling, and for two years gave up his Missionary Baptist affiliations and worked in his mother's church, the African Methodist. At the end at this period, however, he returned to his father's Baptist faith, and until about 1950 he was in the Birmingham area preaching and working days in an iron strip mine. His father had been head of schools in Selma and Tuscaloosa during these years and Skip spent much of his time with his parents. He was also alone for long stretches. As he has said, he was an only child so he "...always likes to be alone."

In 1951 he returned to Mississippi, going to work as a sharecropper. His mother had died and his father had remarried and was living again in Birmingham. A few years later Skip had become a field hand and was living with his wife Mable in a cabin outside of Dundee, in Tunica County. He was no longer working in the church, and he had given up music. His father died in April, 1963, and he was in Birmingham for the funeral, staying with his step-mother in the house on 15th Way, S.W., for a few days; then he went back to his life as a field laborer.

During this period, however, the interest in the delta blues had grown, and intensive efforts were being made to find the singers who were still living. Gayle Dean Wardlow, the young Mississippian who had traveled with Bernard Klatzko on the trip tracing Patton's backgrounds in the summer of 1963, learned, in the late spring of 1964, that Skip had been raised in Bentonia. Wardlow was still in classes; so he was unable to get to Bentonia for a few weeks, but he had already found another blues man from the early period, Ishman Bracey, living in Jackson, and he told Bracey that he had found a lead to James. While Wardlow was finishing his classes John Fahey, Bill Barth, and Henry Vestine drove to Jackson from California and found Bracey's name in the Jackson telephone directory. Bracey told them that he'd heard Skip was from Bentonia, and they began driving the same afternoon, without even taking time to stop and see Bracey. It took only three inquiries in Bentonia before they'd located a cousin, Martha Polk, who had seen Skip at the funeral in Birmingham the year before. The next day they found Skip in the Tunica County Hospital convalescing from a stomach operation.

Within a few days of his release from the hospital Skip was brought from the South to live in the empty house in Newport, Rhode Ireland, that had been turned over to the blues singers for the 1964 Newport Folk Festival. He was quiet, withdrawn from the others, a slight, thoughtful man, his hair graying, his face guarded. He was still weak from the operation, and he had done only a little playing; but he seemed ready to perform, even though he had only three of his old numbers ready and a new piece that he'd written while he was in the hospital. It was at a blues workshop on a cold and damp Saturday afternoon that he finally sang, along with most of the other blues men who had come up from the South for the Festival. He sat expressionless as he waited to be introduced, but as he stepped slowly onto the small wooden platform to sit down he was trembling and nervous. From behind him on the platform, after introducing him to the three thousand people sitting under gray skies on the wet grass in front of the stage, it seemed as though he might not even be able to sing. His first notes as he began his guitar introduction were fumbled and incoherent; then his left foot suddenly began tapping, the guitar introduction emerged as the old cross-note picking of "Devil Got My Woman," and his voice rose in the same clear falsetto he had used on his recording thirty-four years before. When he finished there was a long, excited roar of applause.

Later in the afternoon Skip sat on a cot in one of the shadowy rooms of the house where he was staying, leaning against a window, playing the guitar for a handful of people who had come back with him from the concert. The sun had fallen below the clouds and there was a lingering, pale sunset behind him as he bent over to show something to one of the boys sitting near him. "See, there's nothing hard to it. You can do it if you try a little." It was clear, from his smile, that he had come back to the blues for good. Despite a recent operation for cancer and the difficulties any of the older blues men has in making a living, he has been playing steadily, and like the Skip James of 1930, he has continued to develop his art into an even more unique expression of the complex patterns of his life.

SKIP JAMES

Photo by Ann Charters

JAYBIRD COLEMAN
Courtesy of Pat Cather

CHARLEY PATTON

TOMMY JOHNSON

ISHMAN BRACEY

B.K. TURNER, "BLACK ACE"

BOOKER WHITE   Courtesy of John Fahey

BERTHA LEE PATTON   Photo by Ann Charters

WILLIE DOSS

Photo by Ann Charters

5. ROBERT JOHNSON

... I was living on, I believe it was 2320 Carr Street during that time and I was playing at Ernest Walker's "House Party" on Jefferson. Robert Johnson had ome over to find me, and he was a stranger in the town so he told me, "Look, I've heard about you." He was just traveling through and he says, "Where you working at tonight?" so I told him and he says, "Can I come over?" and I said "Yeah," so he come over to Walkers'...

Well, we sat in the back yard and that fellow, he went over some guitar and I thought, well, this guy's got it. I mean he was amazing. I was a little bit older than him, but I didn't think anybody had any seniority over me on the guitar, but this guy made me look little. During the time I was fixing to leave town, really, and he played for Ernest Walker for about three weeks and I came back and he stayed with me another week over there, for a very small scale, of course. He held the job until I came back and the truth is it was Robert's job when I came back. Robert continued until he was ready to leave; then the boss put me back to work. Robert was very decent about it, I mean we worked together, but as far as the job was concerned it belonged to Robert ... I don't really know where he was going when he left. He said he was going to Chicago...[1]

Henry Townsend, a blues musician from St. Louis, sitting in his front room on a hot summer night in 1962, thinking back to the first time he'd met Robert Johnson in 1935. In towns up and down the Mississippi River, through the delta, and west into Texas many local singers must have had this same glimpse of Robert Johnson. The thin, guarded teen-ager who stood in their doorway telling them that he'd heard of them. Then in a club or at a neighborhood party he sat down with a guitar and played them into the floor. Townsend called Robert - as a musician "aggressive." Johnson was more than aggressive, he was on fire with his music. Even Son House, who knew him when he was still a boy, and taught him some of the pieces that he recorded, remembers him with some uneasiness.[2.]

... we'd all play for the Saturday night balls and there'd be this little boy standing around. That was Robert Johnson. He was just a little boy then. He blew a harmonica and he was pretty good with that, but he wanted to play a guitar. When we'd leave at night to go play for the balls, he'd slip off and come over to where we were. His mother and step-father didn't like for him to go out to those Saturday night balls because the guys were so rough. But he'd slip away anyway. Sometimes he'd even wait until his mother went to bed and then he'd get out the window and make it to where we were. He'd get where Willie and I were and sit right down on the floor and watch from one to the other. And when we'd get a break and want to rest some, we'd set the guitars up in the corner and go out in the cool. Robert would watch and see which way we'd gone and he would pick one of them up. And such another racket you never heard! It'd make the people mad, you know. They'd come out and say, "Why don't y'all go in there and get that guitar away from that boy! He's running people crazy with it." I'd come back in and I'd scold him about it. "Don't do that, Robert. You drive the people nuts. You can't play nothing. Why don't you blow the harmonica for 'em?" But he didn't want to blow that. Still, he didn't care how I'd get after him about it. He'd do it anyway.

Well, he didn't care anything about working in the fields and his father was so tight on him about slipping out and coming where we were, so he just got the idea he'd run away from home. He was living on a plantation out from Robinsonville. On a man's place called Mr. Richard Lellman. And he ran away. Didn't want to work on any farms.

He stayed, looked like to me, about six months. Willie and I were playing again out at a little place east of Robinsonville called Banks, Mississippi. We were playing there one Saturday night and, all of a sudden, somebody came in through the door. Who but him! He had a guitar swinging on his back. I said, "Bill!" He said, "Huh?" I said, "Look who's coming in the door." He looked and said, "Yeah. Little Robert." I said, "And he's got a guitar." And Willie and I laughed about it. Robert finally wiggled through the crowd and got to where we were. He spoke, and I said, "Well, boy, you still got a guitar, huh? What do you do with that thing? You can't do nothing with it." He said, "Well, I'll tell you what." I said, "What?" He said, "Let me have your seat a minute." So I said, "All right, and you better do something with it, too," and I winked my eye at Willie. So he sat down there and finally

88

*got started. And man! He was so good! When he finished,
all our mouths were standing open. I said, "Well, ain't that
fast! He's gone now!"*

*So he hung around about a week or more, and I gave him a little
instruction. Said, "Now, Robert. You going around playing
for these Saturday night balls. You have to be careful 'cause
you mighty crazy about the girls. When you playing for these
balls and these girls get full of that corn whiskey and snuff
mixed together, and you be playing a good piece and they like
it and come up and call you 'Daddy, play it again, Daddy' --
well, don't let it run you crazy. You liable to get killed. " He
must not have paid it much attention. He laughed it off, you
know. I said, "You gotta be careful about that 'cause a lot of
times, they do that; and they got a husband or a boy friend
standing right over in the corner. You getting all excited over
'em and you don't know what you doing. You get hurt." I gave
him the best instruction. So he said, "Okay." Finally, he left
and went somewhere else again with his guitar. We heard a
couple of his pieces come out on records. Believe the first
one I heard was "Terraplane Blues." Jesus, it was good. We
all admired it. Said, "That boy is really going places." So he
left and went out there from Greenwood, Mississippi. Somewhere out in there...*

The name of the plantation was Letterman's plantation, the small town
nearby, Robinsonville in Tunica County, a few miles east of the Mississippi River. An older brother died a few years ago in Robinsonville,
and efforts to trace the rest of the family have been unsuccessful.

Few of the older delta singers realized that the music they had been
singing all their lives could get them out of their weatherbeaten cabins
and away from the squalor and indignity of their lives. But the younger
musicians - Johnson was eleven or twelve years old when the forty-two
year old Charley Patton did his first recording - grew up conscious of
the large audience which was developing for blues both in the South
and in the larger cities of the North. It is difficult even to talk about the
"Robert Johnson style." He was one of the first delta musicians who
listened seriously to recordings. Verses, accompaniment patterns,
melodies, even vocal inflections from recordings by Leroy Carr,
Scrapper Blackwell, Joe McCoy, Willie Newburn, Kokomo Arnold,
and Lonnie Johnson found their way into his own compositions. Even
some of his delta pieces had elements that he'd taken from recordings.

The "32-20" that Robert recorded was taken almost directly from
Skip James' Paramount recording of "22-20," with a guitar accompaniment instead of the piano. He used most of Skip's verses even though
the first verse didn't make a great deal of sense at the time he recorded
it. Skip, recording in a studio in Grafton, Wisconsin, had sung,

> If I sent for my baby, and she don't come,
> If I sent for my baby, and she don't come,
> All the doctors in Wisconsin, he won't help her none.

In his first verse Robert, recording in a hotel room in San Antonio, Texas, remembered to change Skip's line to a more local setting.

> I sent for my baby, and she don't come.
> I sent for my baby, man, and she don't come.
> All the doctors in Hot Springs sure can't help her none.

But in repeating the verse later in the song he forgot and used Skip's line,

> ...All the doctors in Wisconsin sure can't help her none.

With his facile guitar technique Robert was able to pick almost any style that he'd heard, and he was also a fair vocal imitator. On two of his recordings, "Malted Milk" and "Drunken Hearted Man," the singing was very close to Lonnie Johnson's, and on his recordings of delta songs he often sounded like Son House. In many of his finest performances his use of the growl seems to have been an effort to imitate the tone of Son's darker voice. On other pieces there was a falsetto sound that was very reminiscent of Kokomo Arnold, who had begun recording two years earlier. Few artists as young as Robert - he was probably eighteen or nineteen when he began to record - have found a distinctive artistic voice, and he had still not assimilated many of his young enthusiasms when he began to record. But it wasn't the finger work on the guitar neck or his ability to use a little of everyone else's style that has given Robert his place in the development of the delta blues. He also left a small group of recordings that were not only intensely personal, but were also fully realized musical performances. They were also to be, through Muddy Waters and Elmore James, the pivot on which the delta blues turned from a local style, with deep entanglements in the land and its people, to the rhythm and blues style that developed in the northern cities after the Second World War. Of all the voices that he sang in, his own was the strongest.

Even in the songs that he took from his delta background Johnson had an immediacy that was distinctively his own. Every performer with a personal style sings almost as though he watched himself in a mirror. The incidents, the emotions of his life become part of his songs, just as the movement of a hand is reflected in the mirror. Most of the singers, however, stood a few feet away and looked at themselves within their social setting. Johnson was younger, and with the intent concentration of an adolescent, leaned forward until all he could see was the reflection of his own face. The usual pattern for a blues is a group of verses loosely held together by an underlying emotional concern. Most of the verses are standard textual material, usually general comments tied to the particular situation that the singer has described. Patton composed longer blues that were more closely knit, but these were narrative blues, with the figure of the singer grouped with the other figures of the song. For Johnson, there often seemed to be only himself. In Son House's "Preaching Blues," which he taught to Robert, most of the eleven verses, even though they reflected Son's inability to keep the secular and the religious sides of his life separated, were derived from other recordings, they were confused in their imagery, and there was little continuity in their development. But one of the verses reflected a more direct meeting with the emotional realities.

> Now, I met the blues this morning walking just like a man.
> Umh - walking just like a man.
> I said, "Good morning, blues, now give me your right hand."

It was this verse, the most immediate, that Robert chose to use first in his later recording, and he followed it with his own second verse that expressed even more vividly the painful intensity of the moment.

> And the blues grabbed mama child, tore it all upside down.
> Blues grabbed mama child, and they tore me all upside down.
> Travel on, poor Bob, just can't turn you around...

It was only after he had come so close to his own emotions that he could reach out his hand and touch the reflection of his own face that he went on to the generalized verses that took him a step back from the intensity of the experience, and his "Preachin' Blues" went on with,

> The blues am a low down, stickin' gyp.
>   sp. (Preach 'em now.)
> Umh - am a low down, stickin' gyp.
> You ain't never had 'em, hope you never will.

> Well the blues am a achin' old heart disease,
>   sp. (do it now, you goin' do it?)
> But the blues am a low down achin' heart disease.
> Like consumption, killin' me by degrees...

Sometimes as he turned away the break in mood was disappointing. One of the most personal and expressive moments in blues poetry is the opening of his "Hellhound On My Trail." All of the images, the blues falling down like rain on him, the leaves on the trees over his head shaking with the wind, intensified the desperation he felt at the thought of the hellhound trailing him through the day.

> I got to keep moving, I got to keep moving, blues falling
>   down like hail, blues falling down like hail.
> Umh - , blues falling down like hail, blues falling down like hail.
> And the day keeps on 'minding me there's a hellhound
>   on my trail,
>   hellhound on my trail,
>   hellhound on my trail.

When he fell back on ordinary verse material for the second verse it left the sense of a missed poetic opportunity.

> If today was Christmas Eve, if today was Christmas Eve,
>   and tomorrow was Christmas day,
> If today was Christmas Eve, and tomorrow was Christmas day.
>   sp. (Oh, wouldn't we have a time, baby.)
> All I would need my little sweet rider, just to pass the
>   time away,
>   umh, to pass the time away.

The feeling of the immediate in the first verse, however, still hung over the song like a low line of clouds over the levees along the Yazoo River, and it was one of his most effective performances.

It is not surprising that several of his blues began with a line, "Early this morning...," "I'm goin' get up this morning...," "Early this morning when you knocked upon my door," "Well, the blues this morning..." there is no more personal time for someone young and alone than the first gray light of morning, and in these lines there was some of the painful awareness of life of the adolescent Robert Johnson.

"...At the time I met him he was fresh out of Memphis, he'd been playing out there...he was a dark skinned fellow, kind of round shouldered, very small and very young. I thought he must have been teenage. Of course I didn't know whether he was eighteen or seventeen or fifteen, but he was a teenager at that time. But he didn't like the title of being kid. He was a man as far as he was concerned..." Henry Townsend spent only a few weeks around Robert, but he still had a clear memory of him after nearly thirty years. Two Memphis musicians living in Chicago now, Johnny Shines and Walter Horton, wandered with Johnson for nearly two years, and they remember him with rueful affection. Johnny met him in West Helena, Arkansas, about 1933, Shines was seventeen and he thought Robert was a year or so older than he was when they met. Sitting in Johnny's living room on Chicago's south side Walter laughed and said, "You couldn't run with Robert for long; he wouldn't stay in one place." They came up to Chicago together, but Robert drifted out of town just after they'd gotten there. "We were staying someplace –" Shines shook his head as he thought about it, "I don't remember where it was - and he got up in the middle of the night and left. Just like that! I didn't see him for five months." Walter laughed again. "He was that kind of fellow. If anybody said to him 'let's go,' it didn't matter to him where it was they were going, he'd just take off and go. It didn't matter either what time of day or night it was..." Townsend remembered that Robert was guarded. "If he wanted something he would just bring it to you, but the feeling he had deep inside was hard to tell about..." He was also shy. Don Law, the man who recorded Robert for Vocalion Records in San Antonio, asked him to play for a group of Mexican musicians, and he finally played for them facing a wall looking the other way. But there was little shyness in his singing. He sang with the raw openness of a seventeen year old, and many of the songs had an almost tormented cry. Many blues men spent a lot of time thinking about women, but Son House remembers that Robert was driven by sexuality. The relationships at least left Robert with names to use in his songs. His "girl friends" - the term he used in "When You Got A Good Friend" - included Beatrice in "Phonograph Blues," Bernice in "Walking Blues," "Thelma in "I Believe I'll Dust My Broom," Ida Bell in "Last Fair Deal Gone Down," Betty Mae in "Honeymoon Blues," and Willie Mae in "Love In Vain." There is no way of knowing who they were, or if they were anything more to him than someone to spend a few nights with in a new town. The names were usually included in a conventional verse.

I'm goin' write a letter, telephone every town I know.
I'm goin' write a letter, telephone every town I know.
I can't find my Thelma, she must be in East Monroe, I know.

(I Believe I'll Dust My Broom)

At his last session, in a Dallas office building in June, 1937, he even suggested that he was going to marry one of them, Betty Mae.

Betty Mae, Betty Mae, you shall be my wife some day.
Betty Mae, Betty Mae, you shall be my wife some day.
I wants a little sweet girl that will do anything that I say....

Someday I will return with the marriage license in my hand.
Someday I will return with the marriage license in my hand.
I'm going to take you for a honeymoon in some long, long
    distant land.

(Honeymoon Blues)

But the next song of the session was one of the most touching of all the blues love songs, "Love In Vain," and the girl that he mentioned in the song was someone else.

I followed her to the station, with her suitcase in my hand.
And I followed her to the station, with her suitcase in my hand.
Well, it's hard to tell, it's hard to tell, when all your
    love's in vain,
    All my love's in vain.

When the train rolled up to the station, I looked her in the eye.
When the train rolled up to the station I looked her in the eye.
Well I was lonesome, I felt so lonesome, and I could not
    help but cry.
    All my love's in vain.

93

When the train left the station, with two lights on behind,
When the train left the station, with two lights on behind,
Well the blue light was my blues, and the red light was my mind.
    All my love's in vain.

Umh, Willie Mae,
Umh, Willie Mae,
Umh, let me be your -
    All my love's in vain.

After sexuality the most persistent force in Johnson's blues was a brooding presence that he called the "hellhound" or the devil. It seemed to press against him like the heat from the sun in the fields that he hated. Without Johnson to explain the hellhound, it will always be difficult to say what he meant by the image, but it was only in the strong opening verse of "Hellhound On My Trail," that it had a tormenting aspect for him. He was able to sing of the devil with an almost ironic shrug in other blues, even though the insistence with which the image returns suggests that he was troubled by it.

Early this morning, when you knocked upon my door,
Early this morning, when you knocked upon my door,
I said, "Hello, Satan, I believe it's time to go."

...You may bury my body down by the highway side;
    sp. (Babe, I don't care where you bury my body when I'm
        dead and gone)
You may bury my body down by the highway side;
So my old evil spirit can get a Greyhound bus and ride.

                    (Me And The Devil Blues)

In a later verse of "Hellhound" he also mentioned a voodoo powder; so the concern with Satan could be a reference to a belief in the local black magic practices, which still had some hold in the rural areas.

You sprinkled hot foot powder all around my door, all
        around my door.
You sprinkled hot foot powder all around your daddy's door.
It keeps me with a rambling mind, rider, every old place I go,
        every old place I go.

                    (Hellhound On My Trail)

Robert's endless traveling, from Mississippi to St. Louis, Memphis, Arkansas, Louisiana, and Texas, may have been part of the fear and the torment that he described in "Hellhound."

94

He was not involved in the delta landscape as Charley Patton was, but he mentioned a number of delta towns in his blues. Some of them were river towns - Vicksburg, Friar's Point, Jonesboro, and Rosedale - and when Willie Borum, a Memphis singer, heard Robert, he was working in the juke joints along the river, playing in rundown roadhouses for the work gangs building levees along the banks of the Mississippi.

The strongest musical influence on Robert was Son House, despite the other singers and the recordings that he heard. There don't seem to have been the long sessions like Patton had with the young Howling Wolf, but Henry Townsend also said that "...if you just went over something once Robert would get it and play it just as well as you did the next time, he was that kind of fellow." Some of Robert's songs, like "Crossroads Blues," sound very much like something Son would have sung, even to a mention of "my friend poor Willie Brown," but Son doesn't sing - or even remember - a song like it. The young boy sitting in front of the little stage in one of the country dance halls near Robinsonville might have picked up bits of song from Son and changed them to a more immediate and more carefully shaped blues, without Son remembering what he had used for a verse the night before. Despite Patton's strong presence he doesn't seem to have had any influence on Robert's style except for the evocative guitar figures - played with a knife - in Patton's "When Your Way Gets Dark." Johnson used them to suggest the sound of the wind blowing against a shadowed cabin window in "Come On In My Kitchen."

Willie Brown was also playing with Patton and House, and he was considered the best guitar player of the three of them; so it may have been Willie who influenced Robert's more complex guitar style. From House, however, he learned "Preaching Blues," "Walking Blues," "Milkcow's Calf Blues," and "If I Had Possession Over Judgment Day." Despite his changes in melodic material and accompaniment they still had unmistakable elements of Son's style, and sometimes were very similar to the earlier recorded performances that Son did for Paramount in 1930.

Many of these elements of Robert's style were picked up by younger singers; so it was from Son House, through Robert, that the oldest strains of the delta blues became part of the contemporary blues scene. One of the first pieces that Muddy Waters learned when he was beginning to sing was Robert's "Walking Blues," and one of Johnson's melodies - he used it for "When You Got A Good Friend," "Ramblin' On My Mind," "Me And The Devil," and "I Believe I'll Dust My Broom" - was used a number of times by one of the most important of the post war Chicago singers, Elmore James. James was so successful with a new recording of "I Believe I'll Dust My Broom," that it became his theme song, and he named his group the "Broomdusters." Other singers in Chicago, among them John Shines, who did a recording of "Ramblin' " which had a great deal of Robert's sound, were also influenced by the strained, tense music of Robert's blues, and the delta style took root in the new soil like a seed blown in a heavy September wind.

From the older delta singers Robert picked up most of the elements of the classic Mississippi style. He used the open tunings and played with a bottleneck on a number of pieces, as well as finger picking in the lower strings of the guitar. He even used work song sources for blues like "Last Fair Deal Gone Down." He sang with considerable freedom, his voice light and often in falsetto, embellishing the melodic structure with a great deal of variation in both rhythmic phrasing and vocal attack. His blues were often more song-like than the simple melodies of Patton or House, and he used the European diatonic scale for some of his most intense performances. "Hellhound On My Trail" avoids only the sixth in its scale.

Example 15

I got to Keep mov_ing   I got to Keep mov_ing

blues fall_ing down like hail, — blues fall_ing down like hail.

Um — m ————   blues fall_ing down like

hail, blues fall_ing down like hail   and the

day Keeps on 'min_din' me   there's a hell_hound on my trail, —

— hell_hound on my trail, —   hell_hound on my trail.

The harmonies for "Hellhound," however, were less touched by the song-like melody than the scale. There was an outline of the conventional I -IV - V blues verse in his singing, but in the accompaniment the guitar was in unison with the voice through most of the verse, only suggesting a leading tone or seventh in the treble strings. The harmony in the lower strings was an insistent open chord. For the delta pieces that he learned from Son he kept the older pentatonic scales.

Probably Robert was so influential among younger singers because of his guitar style. Son had already developed the accompaniments into an open, freely expressive voice. Robert took from him the openness of the sound, the reiterated bass tone, and the treble melodic figure following the vocal phrase; then he tightened the elements into a more rhythmically insistent accompaniment. For "Walking Blues" his accompaniment had the movement and the tension of a three or four piece blues group.

Example 16

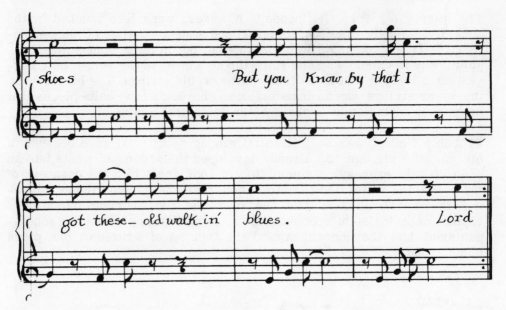

shoes   But you know by that I

got these old walk in' blues.   Lord

Much of the post war Chicago blues was to have this same rhythmic pulse and emotionally vivid singing style.

A salesman for the American Recording Corporation, Ernie Oertle, heard of Johnson, and he brought him to Don Law for the San Antonio sessions. Frank Driggs of Columbia Records, who produced the excellent reissue album of Robert's blues, talked with Law, and much of what Law remembered about Johnson filled in the picture of the young, intensely personal singer that emerged from the recordings themselves. As Driggs wrote,

> " ... *Don Law considered himself responsible for Johnson, found him a room in a boarding house and told him to get some sleep so he would be ready to begin recording at ten the following morning. Law then joined his wife and some friends for dinner at the Gunter Hotel. He had scarcely begun dinner when he was summoned to the phone. A policeman was calling from the city jail. Johnson had been picked up on a vagrancy charge. Law rushed down to the jail, found Johnson beaten up, his guitar smashed; the cops had not only picked him up but had worked him over. With some difficulty, Law managed to get Johnson freed in his custody, whisked him back to the boarding house, gave him forty-five cents for breakfast, and told him to stay in the house and not to go out for the rest of the evening. Law returned to the hotel, only to be called to the phone again. This time it was Johnson. Fearing the worst, Law asked, "What's the matter now?' Johnson replied, 'I'm lonesome." Puzzled, Law said, 'You're lonesome? What do you mean, you're lonesome?' Johnson replied, 'I'm lonesome and there's a lady here. She wants fifty cents and I lacks a nickel...'*"

There was a note of desperation in many of Robert's recordings. Usually if the first take was not acceptable on the second take he often became even more emotionally uncontrolled and the first take had to be used despite the unsteadiness. The desperate emtionalism, the torment of the hellhound, the sexual insistence all seemed to be an expression of an unvoiced fear that he had only a short time to live. He was dead six months after he recorded in Dallas in 1937, but Son House was surprised that he lived as long as he did, rather than that he died so young. " ... he'd go up to a girl he saw at one of those dances and try to take her off, no matter who was around, her husband or boyfriend or anybody ... " There were many accounts of his death, all of them different. Dick Waterman, one of the group that found Son, was told that at a dance at Greenwood, Mississippi, Robert spent most of the night with one girl; then left with somebody else. The girl he left at the dance followed them outside and stabbed him to death in the road. Some of the older singers think he was poisoned by an older woman after he was unfaithful to her. As Son said, it's hard to know.[3.] " ... The next word we heard was from his mother, who told us he was dead. We never did get the straight of it. We first heard that he got stabbed to death. Next, a woman poisoned him, and then we heard something else. I can't remember what it was now, but it was three different things. Never did just get the straight of it. Close as I can get to it, he was about twenty-three or -four. Very young."

6. BOOKER T. WASHINGTON "BUKKA" WHITE

In the small towns of the delta the jail is usually in the courthouse in the middle of the town square, down in the cellar, or upstairs in part of the second floor. A prisoner there is town property, where anyone can get at him. For any offense, from drunkenness to using the wrong drinking fountain, a Negro could find himself locked up in the run down, foul smelling cells, trying to sleep on a filthy mattress while he waited for someone to come get him out. For worse offenses he could be sent from there to the state farm at Parchman, on Highway 49W south of Clarksdale. The threat of prison hung heavy over the head of any Negro in the delta.

The singers were even more effected by the threat. As they drifted from place to place playing for country frolics on the plantations or for dances in the lonely roadhouses, they were always coming up against the local sheriffs. Mississippi was a "dry" state; so even drinking could get them into trouble. As they traveled along the dusty roads they were without any means of support except their battered guitars, and a county judge could put them on a road gang for six weeks vagracy. If someone's woman came up and began to get friendly at a dance they could find themselves in a sullen, drunken fight. Most of them got by like Patton did, trying to get along with everybody in the area where they did most of their singing, playing for white dances as well as colored, and staying out of the way when any trouble started. But the threat was always there, and all of them sang about it in blues after blues. Charley Patton,

<blockquote>
When the trial's in Belzoni ain't no use screamin' and cryin',
umhuh.
When the trial's in Belzoni ain't no use to scream and cry,
umhuh.
Mr. Ware will take you back to Belzoni jail house alive.
</blockquote>

(High Sheriff Blues)

Son House,

Down South, when you do anything that's wrong,
Down South, when you do anything that's wrong,
Down South, when you do anything that's wrong,
They'll sure put you down on the county farm.

(County Farm Blues)

Reubin Lacy,

Layin' in jail, my back turned to the wall.
And I'm layin' in jail, my back turned to the wall.
And I'm layin' in jail, my back turned to the wall.

(Mississippi Jail House Groan)

Sam Collins,

Lord, she brought me coffee, and she brought me tea.
Lord, she brought me coffee, and she brought me tea.
Fell dead at the door with the jailhouse key.

(The Jailhouse Blues)

For Booker White, the young singer who grew up wanting "... to come to be a great man like Charley Patton," prison was an oppressive reality that drew from him some of his greatest blues.

Booker was born in hill country to the west of the delta. His father, John White, was a fireman on the M & O, and in the late 1880's he left Texas and settled in Houston, Mississippi, the county seat of Chickasaw County, about ninety miles east of Clarksdale. He married a woman named Lula Davis in Houston and Booker, he was named Booker T. Washington, was born on November 12, 1909. He was one of five children. His father took the children to Baptist services, and he was a musician as well, playing both the violin and the guitar. Booker learned to sing in church, and while he was still young his father showed Booker and his sister Etta how to tune the guitar and play a few chords. When he was ten years old - in 1919 - Booker went to live with his uncle, Alec Johnson, on a farm in Grenada, Mississippi. Grenada is the county seat of Grenada County, and is only a few miles from the Yalobusha Rivers, one of the streams that flows into the Yazoo River. In Grenada Booker was in the delta blues country. His uncle had a piano for both his son Buster and for Booker, but Booker was still interested in the guitar, and he managed to get hold of a patched-up instrument. He played it late at night when he thought everybody was sleeping, but his uncle got tired of being wakened by the sound of the music and smashed the guitar. Booker was determined to play though, and he got another instrument. He spent his teens working on his uncle's farm or carrying water for local construction gangs.

101

Except for his interest in the guitar there was little to set Booker apart from other adolescents growing up in the delta. They worked in the fields from sun up to sun down, already hardened men when they were sixteen, able to work for hours in the summer heat or bend over a chopping hoe through a trickling spring rain. But, as Booker said, he was different. "... none of the other boys, they didn't have any idea what I was thinking about." Charley Patton was playing around the plantations when Booker was growing up, and he felt that he wanted to be just like Patton, even though he absorbed little of Charley's blues style. It was Patton as a man, rather than a singer, that drew him. Booker never had much success as a performer, but he never stopped playing, and he was sure enough of himself as an artist that in more than thirty years his style changed as little as the stones scattered along the banks of the Yazoo River.

Booker matured as a singer during the period when the record companies were beginning to use delta artists. Paramount, through H. C. Spears in Jackson, was able to get most of them, but Ralph Peer was also looking for artists for the Victor field studio in Memphis. He worked through local agents whenever possible, and it was a white Mississippian, Ralph Limbo, who finally talked to Booker about recording in the spring of 1930, when Booker was just twenty years old. He still remembers his excitement at the possibility of recording. Limbo told him to meet him at the railroad tracks by Swann Lake on a Monday morning late in May, and Booker was there every morning for a week before. When Limbo drove up he had two white guitar players with him in a new Studebaker, a colored preacher, and a blues singer named Napoleon Hairiston. Limbo had a contract with Peer for sixteen sides by the colored artists, and Booker did fourteen of them, some of them with Hairiston singing or playing second guitar. Booker also did some religious songs, and they managed to find two church women to sing with him. By the time the records were to be released, however, it was clear that the depression was going to get worse, and only four of the sides were issued. There was an advertisement for two of the religious titles, "The Promise True And Grand" and "I Am In The Heavenly Way," Victor V38615, in the Chicago *Defender* on October 11, 1930. "This Sermon Sung for You by Washington White 'The Singing Preacher' with Guitars and Women Singers." The other release, Victor 23295, used one of the titles that Hairiston sang, "The New 'Frisco Train," and a long narrative train piece that Booker half sang, half recited with guitar accompaniment, "The Panama Limited."

He tried to stay in Memphis after his recordings, but there weren't enough jobs for him to support himself. He learned a little on the piano, played some jobs on guitar and harmonica; then after a few months he drifted back to the delta. These were hard years for everyone in the United States, and they were even harder for a young field hand trying to get out of Mississippi. In 1933 he married Nancy Buchauney and went back to farming in West Point, Mississippi, a small crossroads town in Clay County, about thirty miles to the southeast of his old home in

Houston. He was still singing, working with his wife's uncle, a rough singer and harmonica player from Alabama named George "Bullet" Williams, who had recorded for Paramount in 1928. They had a job at a roadhouse outside of West Point in 1934, and the next year he moved to Aberdeen, in Monroe County about twenty miles north of West Point. It was a rough, hard life, and he had to become hardened to survive. The story is confused, but he shot a man in the summer of 1937. He was arrested, but according to Big Joe Williams he was set free "on bond" until his trial. He broke bond and fled to Chicago and managed to get a session with Lester Melrose, who was recording for the American Recording Corporation there. Williams says that the Mississippi sheriff found Booker in the studio and arrested him in the middle of the session. There were only two sides recorded on Thursday, September 2, "Pinebluff, Arkansas" and "Shake 'Em On Down." They were released during the winter on the A.R.C.'s Vocalion label.

His music hadn't done much else to help Booker's harsh life in Mississippi, but it did get him out of Parchman Farm. The Vocalion release sold well enough that the company was interested in recording him again, and Lester Melrose made an effort to get him released after he'd been in Parchman six months. But their first appeal was turned down and Booker spent two years in prison. Now, as he looks back on his years in Parchman, he feels that in some ways he was better off then than he has been for much of his life since. He was a camp musician so he did little work in the fields. As he told Ed Denson, one of the men who found him living in Memphis in 1963 and who interviewed him extensively, "... he received better treatment there than he has often received since." But the songs that he wrote while he was in Parchman and recorded within a few weeks of his release in 1940 reflect the unhappiness he felt at the deprivations of prison life. He recorded for the Folk Song Archive of the Library of Congress while he was still a prisoner. Alan Lomax was in the prison with recording equipment in May, 1939, and he recorded a great deal of material. Booker, however, did only two songs, "Po' Boy" and "Sic 'em Dogs On Down." It may have been that he was consciously keeping his songs to himself, waiting until he could get out of the prison farm and into a recording studio. A.R.C. was finally able to get him released after he'd served two years of his sentence. On Thursday March 7, and Friday March 8, 1940, he went into the Chicago studio with a washboard player - probably the studio musician George Washington, who used the names Oh Red or Bull City Red - and recorded twelve titles, released under the name "Bukka" White on the Vocalion and OKeh labels. It was these blues that were shaped in the desperation of his months in Parchman Farm.

Booker has always been a literal blues artist. He uses few of the poetic symbols of a Robert Johnson or a Son House. He had some of Charley Patton's feeling for the local and the direct, although his language was often more halting and prosaic. The two years in Parchman didn't change his blues style, but they intensified the emotional expression of his music. His literalness could have been a limiting factor in his development as a singer, but because he had the experience of Parchman to describe, his direct and barren style took on a richer coloration. In a song like "When Can I Change My Clothes," the repetitiveness of the simple idea would have limited the effectiveness of a blues concerned with conventional eroticism. But "When Can I Change My Clothes" was about his first days in Parchman, and the simplicity of the text and the return again and again to the same idea, intensified his description of the emotions he felt at looking down and finding himself in prison clothes.

> I never will forget that day when they had me in Parchman Jail.
> Wasn't nobody would come and go my bail.
> I wonder how long before I can change my clothes,
> I wonder how long 'fore I can change my clothes.
>
> So many days I would be standing down,
> I would be standing down looking down at my clothes.
> I wonder how long before I can change my clothes.
> I wonder how long 'fore I can change my clothes.
>
> So many days when the day would be cold
> They would carry me out into rain and cold.
> I wonder how long before I can change my clothes.
> I wonder how long 'fore I can change my clothes.
>
> So many days I would be walking down the road,
> I could hardly walk with looking down on my clothes.
> I wonder how long before I can change my clothes.
> I wonder how long 'fore I can change my clothes.
>
> Never will forget that day when they taken my clothes,
> Taken my (civilian clothes?) and throwed them away.
> I wonder how long before I can change my clothes.
> I wonder how long 'fore I can change my clothes.

"High Fever Blues" had the same simplicity of idea as he sang about a prison illness, but it also had the sense of deprivation as he sang "They don't allow my lover come and take my hand." Even the use of the word "lover" had a poignancy. Booker was one of the few blues singers to use this term of endearment when he spoke of his wife.

> I'm sinkin' down with the fever, and it won't let me sleep.
> I'm sinking down with the fever, and it won't let me sleep.
> It was about three o'clock before he would let me be.
>
> I wish somebody would come and drive my fever away.
> I wish somebody come and drive my fever away.
> This fever I'm having sure is in my way.
>
> This fever I'm having sure is hard on a man.
> This fever I'm having sure is hard on a man.
> They don't allow my lover come and take my hand.

I wonder what's the matter with the fever sure is hard on a man.
I want to know what's the matter, how come this fever is hard
　　on a man.
Lord, they say it ain't the fever, just your lover has another man.

Doctor, get your (fever guage?) and put it under my tongue.
Doctor, get your (fever guage?) and put it under my tongue.
The doctor says all you need your lover in your arms.

I wants my lover come and drive my fever away.
I wants my lover come and drive my fever away.
Doctor says you do me more good than he would in all his days.

Even when the blues was not directly concerned with his prison experience it reflected the obsessions of the men, like him, locked behind
the lines of barbed wire in the Parchman enclosure. They worried about
their families, about their women, they built eleaborate fantasies about
their lives outside of prison, they even dreamed of their own deaths.
Booker sang about an effort to find his mother's grave in "Strange
Place Blues," about his imagined death in "Fixin' To Die," and in one
song, "Sleepy Man Blues," suggested some of the emotional defenses
he was able to erect in himself to keep the prison experience from
destroying him.

When a man gets troubled in mind he want to sleep all the time.
When a man gets troubled in mind he want to sleep all the time.
He know if he can sleep all the time his trouble won't worry his
　　mind,
　　　　　　　　　　　　　　　　Won't worry his mind.

I'm feeling worried in mind and I'm trying to keep from crying.
I'm feeling worried in mind and I'm trying to keep from crying.
I am standing in the sunshine to keep from weakening down,
　　　　　　　　　　　　　　　　Keep from weakening down.

I want somewhere to go, but I hate to go to town,
I want somewhere to go to satisfy my mind.
I would go to town, but I hate to stand around.
　　　　　　　　　　　　　　　　Hate to stand around.

I wonder what's the matter with my right mind, my mind keepin'
　　sleeping all the time.
I wonder what's the matter with my right mind, my mind keepin'
　　sleeping all the time.
But when I had plenty money my friends would come around,
　　　　　　　　　　　　　　　　Would come around.

If I had my right mind I would write my woman a few lines.
If I had my right mind I would write my woman a few lines.
I will do most any old thing to keep from weakening down,
　　　　　　　　　　　　　　　　Keep from weakening down.

The blues from these sessions have a disturbing effect. The melodies he used were bare in their outline, like the stripped limbs of an autumn tree, and the verses, with their insistent repetitions, drummed into the ear. The conventional pattern for the development of a blues is from a verse describing the particular situation - what has happened to the singer - to generalized verses commenting on the vagaries of life and love, or loneliness and the blues. Usually for the final verse there is a return to the particular emotions that began the set of verses. Booker, however, with his concern for the literal statement, tended to avoid abstractions and generalized verses. He usually left his occasional narrative material for songs like "Special Streamliner," a spoken description with guitar accompaniment of a train trip. This left him only a limited area of poetic movement, and he usually went from verse to verse with slow, hesitant steps. Other singers were able to turn from side to side as they moved through a blues, using verses that were only tenuously related, and often by this juxtaposition of material they were able to suggest a larger emotional dimension than the five or six verses of the song could have described with a more literal context. But Booker chose to remain within the limits of his opening verses, sometimes restricting even his choice of words and rhymes to two or three sounds repeated over and over again through the song. The blues that he created were often strikingly original, but for someone used to the larger abstractions of the more conventional blues his literalness was disconcerting. Sometimes he began with a conventional statement of his emotional attitude and its cause, as in "Black Train Blues."

> My heart is filled with pain, I believe I'll catch the train.
> My heart is filled with pain, I believe I'll catch the train.
> The one I love, she love another man.

But his second verse moved only a step in developing this idea,

> Yonder come the train, and I got no change.
> Yonder come the train, and I got no change.
> All I can do, just stand and wring my hands.

and in the next verse he moved so slowly in developing his idea that he even repeated the last phrase of the preceding verse.

> I don't feel 'shamed standing and wringing my hands at the train.
> I don't feel 'shamed standing and wringing my hands at the train.
> I ain't the first man the train left cold in hand.

The rhyme patterns have also been tightly controlled "train, man" "change, hands" "train, hand" and the rhyme sounds themselves have an uncomfortable dissonance.

In "Good Gin Blues" the rhymes were even more limited, rhyming gin with again, in, gin, and men.

106

Good morning friend, I wants a drink of gin.
Good morning friend, I wants me a drink of gin.
'Cause they told me this morning revenue men would be back again.

Oh, listen you men, don't you let 'em in.
Listen you men, don't you let 'em in.
Well, they might catch me with a pint of gin.

Oh, come in friends and have a drink of gin,
Come in friends and have a drink of gin.
I know it is a sin, but I love my good old gin.

Oh, come back friends when I have my gin.
Come back friends when I have my gin.
'Cause I don't care nothing about for them old revenue men.

If the individual songs were limited, the twelve blues - "Black Train Blues," "Strange Place Blues," "When Can I Change My Clothes?" "Sleepy Man Blues," "Parchman Farm Blues," "Good Gin Blues," "High Fever Blues," "District Attorney Blues," "Fixin' To Die Blues," "Aberdeen Mississippi Blues," "Bukka's Jitterbug Swing," and "Special Stream Line" - in their interrelationships were a major statement of blues themes and attitudes. It was almost as though Booker had chosen to limit each song so that its sparseness and uniqueness would give it a stronger emotional tie to the other songs he had grouped together for the session. Rather than using the generalizations within each song he outlined a larger reality in the entire group of songs, and the twelve blues have a vivid effectiveness.

The singing style for these sessions was more barren and austere than the singing on the single release he had done for A.R.C. two and a half years before. The recordings had the taste of a raw March wind across the Parchman fields. They were mentioned only briefly in one of the Negro newspapers, the *Amsterdam News* in New York in July, 1940. By the time they were released, the last of the classic delta recordings to be released on a commercial market, the big swing bands had taken over most of the popular music world, Charlie Parker and Dizzy Gillespie were slowly building the vocabulary of progressive jazz, and the blues groups in Chicago were beginning to sound more and more like small swing bands. The reviewer didn't even think the releases were blues. Instead he gave them a sentence describing them as "folk music."

Chicago, St. Louis, Memphis, Baltimore. Booker tried to stay out of the delta. He stayed in Chicago for six or seven months after the sessions, then moved to Memphis. During the war years he traveled to jobs around the country. In 1944 his first daughter, Irene, was born; then in 1946 his wife died of ptomaine poisoning on a trip back home to Mississippi. For a time he tried Chicago again, even recording there with a rhythm and blues band as a guitarist in 1952 or 1953, but he was more or less tied to Memphis. His cousin B. B. King had come to town

MARSHALL — TATE — PANOLA — LAFAYETTE — YALOBUSHA — CALHOUN — CHICKASAW — MONROE — LEE — ITAWAMBA — UNION — PONTOTOC — PRENTISS — GRENADA — WEBSTER — CLAY — LOWNDES — MONTGOMERY — CHOCTAW — OKTIBBEHA — CARROLL — ATTALA — WINSTON — NOXUBEE — LEAKE — NESHOBA — KEMPER

Cove's Sta. — Palestine — Holly Springs — Ashland — TIPPAH — Antioch — Menzi — Coldwater — Wall Hill — Independence — Pine Grove — Austerlitz — Ripley — Union Mills — Lonestar — Dry Run — Old Cairo — Booneville — Arkabutla — Orion — Waco — Pott's Camp — Hickory Flat — Blue Mountain — Orizaba — Dumas — Burnt Mills — Strayhorns — Thyatira — Coleman — Lebanon — Tacaleeche — Guyton — Cotton Plant — Brown's Creek — Burton — Poplar — Senatobia — Waterford — Chulahoma — Bethlehem — Beulah — Molino — Graham — Geeville — Elma — Looxahoma — Tyro — Law's Hill — Nicksville — Cornersville — Baker — Keown V. Hickory Plains — Hazel Dell — Strattons — Glenville — Harmontown — Darden — Myrtle — Baldwyn — Corona — Marietta — Melrose — Como Depot — Abbeville — New Albany — Bruceville — Wallerville — Guntown — Pleasant — Peach Creek — Sledgeville — Maple Springs — Fredonia — Ellistown — Raper — Yoc — Grove Star Place — College Hill — Caswell — Walton — Fairview — Birmingham — Saltillo — Sardis — Oxford — Liberty Hill — Poplar Springs — Macedonia — Pine Spring — Pleas — PANOLA — Tallahatchie — Cora — Denmark — Esparanza — Cherry Creek — Cedar Grove — Mantachie — Batesville — Springport — Yocona — LaFayette Springs — Bruce — Pontotoc — Chesterville — Tupelo — Mooreville — Fulton — Central Academy — Reynolds — Taylor — Dixie — DeLay — Toccopola — Coonewar — Verona — Boland's — Card — Courtland — Eureka Springs — Orwood — Paris — Dallas — Mud Cr. — Algoma — Troy — Eureka — Bigby Fork — Pope's — Elliott's Mill — Spring Dale — Randolph — Shannon — Smithville — Splung — Water Valley — Sarepta — Red Land — Houlka — Central Grove — Tubbs — Dickson — Banner — Matthews — Money — Yota — Okolona — Cotton Gin Port — Oakland — Pine Valley — Reid — Cherry Hill — Quincy — Tillatoba — Air Mount — CALHOUN — CHICKASAW — Aberdeen — Coffeeville — Cotton Valley — Elzy — Houston — Buena Vista — Egypt — Prairie Sta. — Temperance — Torrance — Pittsborough — Cole's Creek — Benela — Erin — Sonora — McCondy — Hill — Hamilton — Hardy Sta. — Yann's Mill — Big Creek — Sparta — Barrs — Muldon — Rees Store — Cascilla — Junction — Grenada — Sabougla — Hopewell — Atlanta — Robertson — Palo Alto — Border Springs — Williamsville — Graysport — Slate Spring — Bently — Hohenlinden — Dixie — Montpelier — Abbott — Vinton — Felix Providence — Cadaretta — Monte Vista — Pine Bluff — Big Springs — Siloam — West Point — Elliott — Redding — Embry — Spring Cr. — Cumberland — Cairo — Waverly — Sweatman — Bellefontaine — Anderson — Line Cr. — Tampico — Smith's Mills — Eskridge — Duck Hill — Alva — Walthall — Henryville — Cedar Bluff — Columbus — Valley Hill — Sawyers — Lodi — WEBSTER — Starkville — Rex — Ash Creek — Tilbee Sta. — Winona — Greensborough — Spring Valley — Steele's Mill — Hickory Gr. — Mayhew's — MONTGOMERY — Mayfield — PAC. — La Grange — Double Springs — Artesia — Cobb Switch — Carrollton — Kilmichael — Bankston — Bywy — Dido — Agricultural College — Westport — Hemingway — Poplar Creek — CHOCTAW — Chester — Wilcox — OKTIBBEHA — Bradley — Sessumsville — Trinity — Blackmonton — GOMERY — Huntsville — Whitefield — Choctaw Agency — 62 Mile Siding — Vaiden — Liddell — French Camps — Snowville — Ennis — Oktoc — Crawford — Black Hawk — Brock — Irvingville — Coniceville — New Prospect — Pugh — Allgood's Mill — Deerbrook — Emory — West — Beatty — Mitchell's Mills — Spay — Webster — Loakfoma — Brookville — Cliftonville — Brazelia — McGee's — Durant — Hesterville — Wells — Barksdale — Singleton — NOXUBEE — Prairie Point — Gray's Mill — Kosciusko — Newtonville — Thompsonville — Perkinsville — Hamby — Macon — Kosciusko Jc. — WINSTON — Louisville — Rome — Randall's Bluff — Mashulaville — Goodman — Sallis — Wamba — Noxapater — Fearn's Springs — Cooksville — New Port — Centre — Coopwood — Handle — Gholson — Shuqualak — Cuba — Vowell — Plattsburgh — Aden — Wahalak — Binnsville — Oak Ridge — Yorka — North Bogue — Chitto — Prince — Kellis' Store — Couparle City — Thomastown — Palona — Coosa — Remus — Lake Burnside — North Bend — Kemperton — Peden — Scooba — Kirkwood — Conway — Edinburgh — Philadelphia — Coffadeliah — KEMPER — Camden — Carthage — LEAKE — Laurel Hill — NESHOBA — Pea Ridge — Mount Nebo — De Kalb — Ofahoma — Colah — Milldale — Watkinsville — Cushtusa — Moscow — Sugar — Sulphur Springs — Lamenta — Madden — Dixon — Tucker — Herbert — Oak Grove — Narkeeta — Millville — Standing Pine — Tuscola — Java — Texas — Chickasahay — Sharon — Estesmill — Walnut Gr. — Beech Springs — Ft. Stephens — Jacksonville — Tamola — Good Hope — Lena — DISON — Canton — Ludlow — Cash — Damascus — New Ireland — Lucerne — Daleville — Rushing's — Lauderdale — Horaceville — Harpersville — County Line — Battlefield — Mount Vernon — Union — Sta.

and Booker helped him get started as a singer. He was working days at a tank factory, living in a boarding house in Orleans Street, and working occasional jobs with another older singer, Frank Stokes.

Despite his wanderings, however, he had thought of Aberdeen, Mississippi, as his home during the years that he was in prison, and in his "Aberdeen, Mississippi Blues" he had sung "Aberdeen is my home, but the mens don't want me around ..." After a letter to Avalon, Mississippi, in 1963 had led to the rediscovery of Mississippi John Hurt, John Fahey, a young guitarist who was studying at the University of California in Berkeley, wrote to "Booker T. Washington White (Old Blues Singer), c/o General Delivery, Aberdeen." Relatives sent the letter on to Booker a month later, and he wrote to Fahey. Two hours after his letter reached Berkeley, Fahey and another blues enthusiast who was a graduate student at the University, Ed Denson, left for Memphis. They found him in his rooming house, found that he still played, recorded him that first afternoon, and a few weeks later released a long playing record of the session.

There had always been a feeling of strength in Booker's recordings, and the new material made it clear that the strength had grown from his belief in his music. There had been almost no change in style in the thirty-five years that had passed since he began recording. There had been a slight easing of the harshness of his singing for the 1937 A.R.C. session, a suggestion of the popular style of Big Bill Broonzey in the phrasing, and there was a second guitar to soften the sound of his delta open tuning. But in 1964 he was just as he had been in 1930, 1939, and 1940. He even did the song "Po' Boy" that he had recorded for Alan Lomax while he was still in Parchman, a sentimental country song played at a fast tempo with a difficult and complex guitar accompaniment. In 1964, as "Poor Boy Long Ways From Home," the song and the accompaniment were almost unchanged from the earlier version, and there was the same excitement in the strong voice and the guitar picking. He still accompanied it in an open G tuning, D, G, D', G', B, D'', using a knife on the strings with the guitar flat across his lap. There was no longer the tension and the emotional force in the verses, but the songs he recorded for Denson and Fahey were a strong and individual musical statement.

Booker's music is almost an archetypal delta blues style. He sings in the middle of his voice with the tone dark and harsh, and like Patton he tends to move melodically in intervals of a third or fourth, with the interval clearly defined and little vocal embellishment. The accompaniments are very strong, impatient and hard. They are unvarying in their emphasis, usually repetitive patterns of notes played with his thumb on the lower strings and a melody played on the upper strings, generally with a metal ring on the little finger of his left hand. He uses the open E tuning as well as the standard tuning, and as with most delta singers, in the open tunings the harmonies in the bass strings, usually played with an alternate thumb picking, are unchanging. To lighten the heaviness of the accompaniment he tends to sing with considerable rhythmic freedom against it, and his literal concerns within the verse often lead him into lines of very irregular lengths. He often seems to be almost speaking the verses instead of singing them. Few singers have made so little change in the rhythmic patterns of their speech and singing. Because of this even the relentless drive of his accompaniment has to yield to the irregularities of the line, and his phrase patterns vary considerably within a song, sometimes using measures of 5/4 and 2/4 in a generally 4/4 context.

Example 17

(Sleepy Man Blues)

Often he is as restricted with melody as he is with rhyme, but the loose construction of the verbal rhythms makes it possible for him to work within his small limits and still be effective. In his first recording of "Aberdeen, Mississippi Blues" he used only four notes in the vocal line, but the verse was rhythmically very free, as though he were compensating for the melodic barrenness.

Example 18

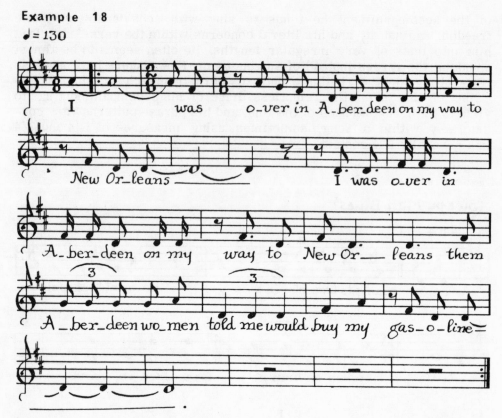

Booker went on to California with Fahey and Denson, and for a few months tried to make a living as a singer. There was further recording, and sessions with Chris Strachwitz for his Arhoolie Record Company in Berkeley. Strachwitz has always used a great deal of imagination in his recording projects and he let Booker extend his songs into lengthy blues stories. On the albums, called "Bukka White, Sky Songs", Booker generally returned to older melodies - "Aberdeen, Mississippi Blues" was used as the melody for "Alabama Blues," "Special Streamliner" for "Bald Eagle Train," "Po' Boy" for "Jesus Died On The Cross To Save The World" - but he improvised new sets of verses. A number of other singers do this, among them Lightning Hopkins and George Montgomery in St. Louis, but they use more generalized material. Lightning often is able to extend his improvisations into effective emotional statements, with considerable use of elaborate poetic imagery. Booker was as literal in the "sky songs" - as he said, "I just reach up and pull them out of the sky - call them sky songs - they just come to me." - as he had been in the 1940 sessions after he'd left Parchman, but without the intensity of the Parchman experience to limit and direct his material, he became diffuse and vague, the verses often contradictory and their narrative movement chaotic. But Strachwitz also recorded a rambling folk tale which he called "Mixed Water," Booker's reminiscences of his early experiences playing the blues against his grandmother's wishes. It was often fresh and engaging and in it Booker was able to talk more freely than he was in the more confining song forms.

There were some jobs for Booker in the first few weeks, mostly at a coffee house called the Cabale on San Pablo Avenue in Berkeley, but it was difficult for him to find an audience for his music. Booker was too strong for his audiences, too strong and too intense, and his songs were too unrelenting. Finally he was left alone in Los Angeles to finish an engagement at a local coffee house. On one of his last nights a young folk singer who had befriended him came to his room to say goodbye. Aware that when the boy left he would have to face the emptiness of the Los Angeles night he suddenly began telling a story, using his hands and his voice to imitate the people he was describing. The story began a little after two in the morning, and when he'd finished it was four hours later and the dawn was breaking. Then, just as he'd done after his sessions, he began to pack to make his way back to Memphis. There have been a few jobs on the East Coast in recent years and some festival appearances, but his music has still not gotten him out of his hard life of rooming houses and laboring jobs.

7. MISSISSIPPI - THE COUNTRY SINGERS

Most of the roads through the delta have been paved in the last twenty years, and the black asphalt surface winds across the flat landscape soft and heavy with tar smells in the summer heat; but the mud roads still lead off toward the sluggish creeks and the back waters along the Mississippi. Through the thin trees there is the drifting haze of a wood fire in a cabin stove and paths worn into the dirt by children's bare feet. Beside the cabins the ground has been cleared and in the ragged furrows there is usually a stand of half-grown cotton or rows of summer corn, against a rusting wire fence some hills of beans, peas, squash, the vines straggling over the burned earth. Through the 1920's and the 1930's the blues grew and spread through the Mississippi countryside, and there was a crowded growth of local styles and singers. More and more of the bluesmen left Mississippi for the slums of West Chicago and Detroit as the 'thirties lengthened, but in the 'twenties nearly every cluster of cabins strung out along a plantation road had someone who played the guitar and sang for dances and parties on Saturday night.

Until the commercialization of the blues in the 'thirties there was no weeding or thinning of the local styles, and there was so much recording of the delta music that it is possible to make rough groupings of many of the singers into stylistic areas or influences. Before the period of recording began the styles grew like the weeds along the road, a few men on a plantation, two or three singers in one of the small towns sitting in a crowded room with a bottle of corn whiskey, their shirts soaked with perspiration, following each others' fingers on the neck of the guitar. Even in the delta counties, with their scattering of farms on the back roads, the styles were often highly individual, but there was a tendency for a few men to cluster around a strong creative personality.

Sometimes on the land behind one of the weathered cabins corn and beans were planted together and the vines grew up around the young cornstalks. From a distance, on one of the paths through the fields, the leaves looked

114

like a green tangled mass. It is just as difficult now, after thirty-five years, to untangle Willie Brown from Charley Patton and Son House. Bertha Lee Patton couldn't even describe him without relating him to the other two. "He was shorter than they were, but thicker ..." It was the same for his guitar playing. "Willie was a better guitar player than Charley was, Son House, too. At least he thought so, and they thought so too." When Son House, Willie's closest friend, tried to talk about his playing, like Bertha Lee he had to describe his playing in comparison with Charley's. "Oh, he could beat Charley. Now, you want to hear that 'Pony,' you think Charley can do it good, he's (Willie) the one. They used to fall out about the 'Pony'..."[1.]

Both Charley and Son liked to use Willie as a "commentor" - someone who "kept their spirits up..." when they were recording. Willie's voice was on some of Charley's records, and he played second guitar for Charley on the last two sessions for Paramount late in 1929 and in the summer of 1930, but he did only four pieces of his own, "M and O Blues," "Future Blues," "Kicking In My Sleep Blues," and "Window Blues." Of these only "M and O Blues" and "Future Blues" have been found. In both of the songs there was some of Charley's presence in the voice and the phrasing. Willie's voice was stronger, with a darker quality, but "Future Blues" was another version of Charley's distinctive "Moon Going Down" melody, and "M and O Blues" was closely related to elements in the style of Son House, as well as other Mississippi singers like Kid Bailey and Tommy Johnson. There was assertiveness, the insistence of someone singing to be heard, in Willie's style, but that also was characteristic of Patton. It was in his guitar accompaniments that he emerged most distinctly as a creative performer, even though there were similarities between their instrumental techniques. The accompaniment of "Future Blues" was a brilliantly realized concept, complex, musical, and expressive, similar to the accompaniments that Patton used for the same melody - "Moon Going Down," "High Water Everywhere," "Screamin' And Hollerin' The Blues" - but more carefully developed. It was the "second" part that he had used for his accompaniments with Charley, and that Charley had used, with a number of variations, for his solo versions of the melody. For the accompaniment the guitar was tuned to an open G chord, d-g-d-g-b-b, and the style used both finger picking - in the opening descending pattern - and a strum on the open strings - at the end of the second line. The accompaniment for "M and O Blues" was conceived within a different rhythmic framework and used a different tuning - an open E chord - so it is likely that the two still undiscovered pieces, "Kicking In My Sleep Blues" and "Window Blues," will also be in different accompaniment styles. It will be difficult to evaluate Brown's musical contribution to the delta blues until they have finally been found, but although he seems to have been in Patton's shadow for much of his musical career, he had developed his own style from the strongly rooted delta music.

Because of Willie's close relationship with Son House, his life is less obscure than the lives of men like Kid Bailey or Blind Joe Reynolds.

He was born in Robinsonville about 1900, and met Charley when they were both young men working on Dockery's Plantation. Son met them about 1928, and he and Willie traveled together until Son decided to try living in the North during the Second World War. He was able to get Willie to stay with him for a short time, but Willie returned to Mississippi and he died there about 1942. [2.]

It was while I was in Rochester that Willie died. After I started working for the New York Central, I was writing and telling Willie about it and eventually I got him to decide that he wanted to come up. So I sent him a ticket and a little money to ride on and he came to Rochester and I got him a job. After a little bit, he sent for his girlfirend, and she came. So one night, we were sitting up talking and she told some things that he didn't think she would. He got mad then and wanted to send her back. He told her to get packed and he told me, "Son, I'm going to leave you the money and I want you to buy her ticket. Not going to trust her. You buy her ticket at the Greyhound and see that she gets on with her suitcase. I don't want to see her when I get off from work and come home." He was living with me. So I got the ticket and she left. Well, soon after that, he wanted to go. Back to a little place about twenty miles outside Memphis. That's where he'd been living before he came to Rochester. I said, "Well, Bill, you going to try and find Rosetta now. Ain't you?" "Aw, naw," he said. I said, "Cut it out. That's what you're thinking about." So he left and went on down.

Well, the first part of the next year, I had a two-week vacation so I went down to see him. He had just had an operation for ulcers, and everytime he'd eat a meal, he'd have to lay down flat on his back for thirty minutes. Well, after the different guys heard I was there, they all wanted me to come and play for them. "Son House's here!" And they gave extra parties and everything, and Willie would go and play with me. The doctors had told him not to drink any more, but he'd be with me and the fellas would come around offering me whiskey, you know. I'd turn it up and Willie would look at me drink it. He knew how we used to do and he'd want a drink so bad. He'd say, "Let me taste a little of that." I'd say, "Bill, you know what the doctors said," He said, "I'm going to try it anyhow. It looks so good." So he'd take little nips, you know.

Well, a couple of weeks after I got back to Rochester, I got a telegram from his girl that Willie was dead. I said, "Well, sir. All my boys are gone." That was when I stopped playing. After he died, I just decided I wouldn't fool with playing any more. I don't even know what I did with the guitar.

116

Patton had an even stronger influence on the music of his accompaniest, the rough country fiddler Henry Sims. For at least two of the four songs he recorded, "Farrell Blues" and "Tell Me Man Blues," he used Charley's "Green River Blues" melody, and on all of his recordings Charley played the guitar accompaniment. The only other influence on his singing seemed to be his own violin style, and his vocal melody closely followed his usual blues solo pattern, despite its angularity and rhythmic stiffness. As Klatzko and Wardlow learned on their trip through the delta, he was also personally closer to Patton than either Willie or Son. [3.]

> *Early Tuesday morning, we left for Farrell. Farrell lies just a few miles west of Clarksdale, near the levees of the Mississippi River. There's a general store just off the main road. Another road divides the cotton fields and the inevitable Negro houses whose occupants care for them. The houses were recessed about 150 yards off the paved road with a dirt road leading to the main group, as well as to a few scattered houses.*
>
> *We had come to Farrell looking for Henry Sims, the primitive country fiddler and singer who recorded four obscure sides under his own name and accompanied Patton on many others during Patton's second session. Pete Whelan had first suggested that Sims might be from Farrell.*
>
> *We approached the first house in a row of houses that made up most of Farrell. A large dark woman in her late middle years came to the porch.*
>
> *After our usual opening with a general discussion of old time blues singers, I asked, "Does Henry Sims live around here?"*
>
> *"Henry Sims lives down in the last house."*
>
> *"Does he play fiddle and sing?"*
>
> *"HUH? Oh, you mean Son Sims. He died about three years ago."*
>
> *"How old was he when he died?"*
>
> *"He was about 67 years old. You know, Son Sims was in the army in World War I."*
>
> *"Did you ever hear of Charley Patton?"*
>
> *"Sure, I seen Patton and Sims playing together around here. Charley died some time ago. Son didn't want to play anymore after that. He took it real bad..."*

117

The record companies who were recording delta singers in the late 1920's and early 1930's were not making an effort to document the local blues styles, but they recorded some of the most individual and creative of the country blues men. The music was developing in such a rich profusion during these years that often the performances went beyond a personal reworking of one of the dominant Mississippi styles, and the singer moved toward a melodic or rhythmic concept that could have been the basis for a whole stylistic development within the blues itself. The blues in this period was a young, still growing song form, and it could sprawl in any direction the singer wanted to try. Often these isolated singers recorded only a handful of sides, but their music still had a tough muscularity. One of these obscure delta men was Garfield Akers, who had begun to move toward a more complex rhythm in his accompaniments. Little is known about his life. He may have been born in Hernando, a small town in De Soto County, just below the Tennessee line about thirty miles south of Memphis on Highway 51. He recorded in Memphis in 1929 and 1930, and finally settled in Memphis where he died about 1962 at the age of sixty. It is possible that he had a son who is still living in Memphis and plays a little in his father's style. The amount of recording that Akers did was almost as slight as the amount of information known about his life. There were four sides, "Cottonfield Blues - Part 1 and 2" recorded in September, 1929, and "Dough Roller Blues" and "Jumpin' And Shoutin' Blues" recorded three or four months later. The melody and the accompaniment style was the same for all of them, except that there was a heavier second guitar on "Cottonfield Blues." The melodic line moved in a series of descending movements from an opening tone a tenth above the fundamental in the accompaniment, and was organized in the conventional three line verse form.

A number of Mississippi men used an accompaniment style for two or three of their pieces that had some similarities to the Texas technique of alternating simple chords under the vocal line with more complex finger picked patterns between the lines. There was a suggestion of this style in the accompaniments of Blind Joe Reynolds, Sam Collins, and Booker White; although in most of their pieces there was a unison melody in the guitar with the vocal phrase. In his accompaniments Akers used a rhythmic variation of this concept, alternating contrasting rhythmic units while still keeping the steady beat beneath the voice. The shifting stresses gave a new impetus to the sung melody. In "Dough Roller Blues" the rhythms alternated in groups of four or six measures; in the other pieces the shift was in smaller groups of two or three measures. One of the rhythms, accompanying the voice, was a simple syncopation,

and the other a more complex unit that was usually,

The complete pattern for the four measure line was,

Within this rhythm the harmonic changes were almost in the standard pattern, I-I-I-I-IV-IV-I-I-V-V-I-I, but the sound of the accompaniment was changed considerably, and the chord movements had less of their rhythmic function. The sound was almost a tonal drumming, and in its repetitive insistence it would have had almost an African sound except for the emphasis on the first and third beats of the measure. The pattern was varied with a beginning phrase in the bass strings of the guitar that he used for at least a verse in each of the pieces. The figure was a series of 8ths through the opening two measures of the accompaniment.

There was also some irregularity in the length of the measures. His singing emphasized the held tones of the line and often he extended the measure to six beats, still keeping the rhythm of the guitar. The guitar measure could be divided into half measure note groups and he used these to fill in the lengthened phrase. His voice was higher in pitch than the heavy tone of Patton or Son House, but it was richer in sound than a voice like Robert Johnson's. Against the rush of the accompaniment it had a strong presence and, despite the use of conventional verse material, his pieces were very effective. Akers had so little opportunity to record that there was only a suggestion in the three blues of the rhythmic concept that he had begun to develop. Only one singer seems to have picked up the style from him, Robert Wilkins, a Memphis singer who grew up in the delta and learned his "Get Away Blues" from Akers. It was unfortunate that so few other bluesmen were able to hear his use of the contrasting beat patterns, since the concept could have helped the later singers to avoid some of the rhythmic monotony that has limited the development of the modern blues. It was, as well, a concept that could give a new dimension to the blues that will emerge from the years of growth and consolidation ahead.

The emphasis on strongly marked rhythms was one of the dominant characteristics of the delta style, and one of the first delta men to record, Williams Harris, based his work on a strongly defined 4/4 rhythm, even though other elements of the Mississippi accompaniment were not fully developed. He had left Mississippi with a medicine show and was in Birmingham in the summer of 1927, when the Gennett Electrobeam studio was working in the city. He did two titles for the company in Birmingham and then went to the Richmond, Indiana studios for three days of recording in October of the next year. On pieces like his "Bullfrog Blues" he used a verse form with a delayed completion of the first line, similar to Patton's fifth verse in "Moon Going Down."

> Have you ever woke up with them bullfrogs on your,
> > bullfrogs on your,
> > bullfrogs on you,
> > I mean mind?
> Have you ever woke up, mama, bullfrogs on your mind?
> Have you ever woke up with them bullfrogs on your mind?

Although the rhythm was in a heavy 4/4 he lightened it with softer afterbeats, using a thumb and finger strum on the guitar, rather than finger picking. As a medicine show singer he did a number of the more conventional blues — his "Hot Time Blues" was an eight bar song with the same chord progression as Papa Charlie Jackson's "Salty Dog,' VI-VI-II-II-V-V-I-I-, but his voice had the delta insistence, and the bare, unadorned melodic outline.

Blind Joe Reynolds, who did four titles for Paramount in 1930, was one of the many delta men who, like Harris and Akers, made only a few recordings, but whose style developed another aspect of the delta music. He was a more impassioned singer than Harris and his half shouted, half sung melodic phrase was nearly arhythmical in its irregularity. The guitar was almost silenced during some of the lines, entering after the voice with heavy figures in the middle strings played with a bottleneck. He used an open tuning, strumming the guitar for some of the accompaniment. Reubin Lacy, who was one of the first singers who influenced Son House, also played with an open tuning, but the rhythm was more regular than Reynold's. He played with the strings very slack, tuning the guitar down to his dark and low voice. On his "Ham Hound Crave," a 1928 Paramount release, there was some Barbecue Bob influence in the repeated lines in the later verses, but his "Mississippi Jail House Groan" was in an almost pure delta style. In the accompaniment he played a dotted eighth note rhythm on the top string and used a descending bass pattern against it. The note on the top string continued almost unchanged through the piece, functioning as a harmonic pedal tone something like the top string of the mountain five-string banjo, which is unfretted. His beat was very slow and deliberate, the only harmonic change in the accompaniment a tonic seventh anticipating the subdominant of the second line, which he sang as though the harmony had changed even though he went back to the tonic after the momentary change to the I7. He made the chord change by dropping the tone on the top string a whole step to the seventh of the scale, then sliding the note back to the tonic. The text was confused, going from a sombre prison mood,

> Layin' in jail, my back turned to the wall.
> And I'm layin' in jail, my back turned to the wall.
> And I'm layin' in jail, my back turned to the wall.

to a half serious sexual boast,

> And my mama told me, my papa told me too,
> And my mama told me, my papa stood and cried,
> You got too many women now for any boy your size,

still with the brooding presence of the slow rhythm and the droning note on the high guitar string.

Although Son House remembers a number of other Mississippi singers like Lacy, he has no recollection of a blues man who was closely related in style to Patton and to Willie Brown. The singer, Mississippi Kid Bailey, did only two sides for Brunswick in 1929, "Mississippi Bottom Blues" and "Rowdy Blues," the "Mississippi Bottom Blues" using Patton's "Moon Going Down Melody" and "Rowdy Blues" Willie Brown's "M And O Blues." The accompaniments were so close to the guitar techniques of the other two men that Son, after listening to the record, feels that it must be Willie on the guitar, even though he's never heard of Bailey. The accompaniment for "Mississippi Bottom Blues" was the higher eighth note pattern that Patton used in his duets with Willie, letting Willie play the descending bass line. Bailey's performance was considerably more relaxed than Patton's, with the steady, lightly swinging beat that was characteristic of the Jackson singer Tommy Johnson. The vocal line was conceived in terms of the entire piece, almost as an adjunct to the accompaniment; so there was considerable displacement of stress in the verse. There was some of this feeling in "Rowdy Blues," the vocal line, as in "M And O Blues," beginning on a subdominant harmony. The accompaniment was in open E tuning. One of the verses that Bailey used even turned up later in Son's 1942 Library of Congress recordings, although Son could have gotten it from a number of other delta singers.

> Did you get that letter I mailed in your back yard?
> Did you get that letter I mailed in your back yard?
> It's sad, it's sad but true, best of friends have to part.

Bailey's voice was strong and rich, and he seems to have been a sensitive and skillful blues man. Just as with Akers and with Rube Lacy and Blind Joe Reynolds it was unfortunate that he had no opportunity to record more than a handful of songs for release as part of the commercial record output of the late 'twenties.

The blues grew in every part of the Mississippi soil, and often the music from the eastern hill country or the southern pine country had moments with the intensity and the drama of the greatest delta music. In the flat sandy country just above the Louisiana line the music was mingled with influences from recordings and from local white singing, but there was still a deep blues presence. It was an elusive mood, like the shadows under the ground pines, but it dominated the singing of one of the few southern Mississippi singers to record extensively, Sam Collins. Little is known about his life, but Dean Wardlow has learned that he was raised in McComb, Mississippi, about fifteen miles above Louisiana in Pike County, and that he died in Chicago in the 1950's. He did his first recording for Mayo Williams in 1927, when Williams had left Vocalion and was trying to set up his own Black Patti label. Collins was one of his first artists, and there was even an advertisement in the Chicago *Defender* for the first release, with a rough drawing of Collins playing the guitar, on July 2, 1927.

> Here he is, Crying Sam Collins and his Git-Fiddle.
> Blues Oh Lawd, "I Mean." Sam cries and weeps out loud,
> does he make his old Git-fiddle weep and moan "And How!"
> Go to your dealer and ask him for -
> Black Patti Record No. 8025
> Jail House Blues, Sam Collins and his Guitar.

He continued to record for more than five years, and he did almost fifty titles, nearly as much recording as Patton did, but only nineteen of his sides were released. The issues were on several labels, most of them cheaper labels for the five and ten cent store record counters. They included Black Patti, Champion, Herwin, Silvertone, Bell, Gennett, Supertone, Banner, Perfect, Conqueror, Melotone, Oriole, and Romeo. The companies used a number of pseudonyms for Collins since each of them was selling the same record at the same time. He was "Big Boy Woods" on Bell, "Jim Foster" on Champion and Silvertone, "Bunny Carter" on Conqueror, and "Salty Dog Sam" on the Banner, Oriole, Perfect, and Romeo releases.

Collins wasn't a creative singer on the level of Son House or Willie Brown, despite the number of titles that he recorded, but there was an intensity in his best work, a brooding sense that fused the awkwardnesses of his style into a whole expression that was often moving. However, much of what he recorded was derivative material, often from country white sources as well as other recordings. Songs like "Hesitation Blues" had the sound of one of the Carolina hillbilly bands like Charlie Poole's, and the prison folk song "Midnight Special," sung in a very high falsetto, had the rhythmic quality of white gospel groups like Ernest Phipps and his Holiness Singers. On "It Won't Be Long" he had some of the hesitations and harmonic uncertainty of the Texas singer Henry Thomas in the same kind of white sentimental songs. His gospel pieces were generally sung with a frailed accompaniment and little change in the verses from the standard song book versions.

Wilson's Point   Rolling Fork   Lake City   Triune   Home Park   Vaughans   Couparle City   Thomast

Alexandria   Mayersville   Campbellsville   Yazoo City   Benton   Deasonville   Camden   Kirkwood

Ben Lomond   ISSA   SHARKEY   Evana   YAZOO   MADISON   Ofah

Providence   Shipland   Watsonia   Doyer   Way's Bluff   Sulphur Springs   Millville

Tallulah   Enola   Woodbine   Vernon   Canton   Sharon   Good Hope

Hay's Landing   Suedes   Satartia   Livingston   Ludlow

Illawara   Arcadia   Halpin's   Dick   Prattville   Calhoun   Goshen Spring   Leesburgh

Omega   Ingomar   QUENA   Phoenix   Madison Sta.   Fannin

Brunswick   Flower ree   Russellville   Bolton's Depot   Clinton   Touga Loo   Lucknow   Armistead Depot

Waverly   Haynes Bluff   Fox Landing   Pelahatchee Depot

Tallulah   Forest   Redwood   Oak Ridge   JACKSON   Spears

WARREN   Home   Cardiff   VICKSBURG   Midway Sta. VICK.   Rowell's   Brandon

Delta   Smith's Sta.   Edward's Depot   HINDS   RANKIN

Mound   Borina   Warrenton   Raymond   Mississippi Spr.   Monterey   Lynwood

New Carthage   Diamond   Oakley   Byram   Steen's Creek   Steep Bank

Palmyra   Goodrum   Auburn   Midway   Cato

Hurricane   Cayuga   Adams   Dry Grove   Braxton

New Town Landing   Rocky Springs   Sta. Chapel Hill   Terry   King

Ursino   Leo   Nanachehaw   Utica   Bear Creek

Grand Gulf   Brook's Landing   White Oak Creek   Harrisville   Dlo Old

ke St. Joseph   B. Pierre   Burtonton   SIMPSON

ound Bayou   Morehead's   Saint Elmo   Crystal Springs   Gatesville

N. Fk.   Myles   McCaleb   Georgetown

Port Gibson   Hermanville   Gallman   Rials

St. Joseph   CLAIBORNE   Linden   Hazlehurst   WESTVILLE   Mount Z

Martin   Mount Hope   COPIAH   Bridgeport   Gwinville

Rodney   Jefferiesville   Rockport   Hebron

Rabbit Harbor   Tillman's Sta.   Martinsville   Tryus   Grange   Jaynesvi

Gum Ridge   Red Lick   Beauregard   West Fork   White Sand

JEFFERSON   Fayette   Caseyville   Wesson   Hooker   Silver Creek

Church Hill   Fowler's   Perth Union Church   Montgomery   Mt. C

Lowenburgh's Sta.   Erwinsville   Brookhaven   LAWRENCE   Blounty

Cannonsburgh   Udbra Friendship   LINCOLN   Fair River   Monticello   Santee

Stanton   Veto   McCall's Cr.   Wilkesburgh

Washington   Hamburgh   Meadville   Chamberlain   Oak Vale   Lightvil

Foster's   Morgan's Fork   Bogue Chitto

ADAMS   Turner's   FRANKLIN   Johnson's Sta.   Sartinville   Col

Hutchin's   Little Springs   Cam

Kingston   Kibbeville   Bunckley   Smithdale   Topisaw

Knoxville   O'Neal's   Zion Hill   Summit   McComb   China Grove

Yeagers   Sera   Merwin   Dickey   Holmesville

Cold Springs   Kahnville   Bates Mill   Quinn   Magnolia   Tyler Town   Walker's Bridge

Kienstra's Store   Wilkinson   AMITE   Hardee's   Dillon   Fordsville

Hudryville   Woodville   Centreville   Liberty   Chataw   Carter's Hill   Live Oak

ort Adams   Holly Retreat   Rose Hill   Gillsburgh   Osyka

Langside   Ashwood Sta.   WILKINSON

Woodland   Palestine   Shady Grove

Burlington   Tangina   Franklinton

Greensburgh   Arcola   Welch's Bridge   Gordontown

Pine Grove   Amite City   Yamac

Independence

MISSISSIPPI   ST. LOUIS   PAC.   NATCHEZ   NEW ORLEANS   CHICAGO

Pearl River   Big Black River   Big Bahala Cr.   West Pearl River   Amite River   W. Fk. Amite River   Tickfaw River   Strong Dolbs Cr.   Greens Cr.

Of all the Mississippi singer Collins was probably the most limited guitarist. He used an open tuning for nearly all of the blues, an e-b-e'-g#-b'-e''- tuning, and his harmonic change was limited to the barred sub-dominant at the fifth fret. He may have done some of his playing with the guitar across his lap, but for the blues it sounds as though he were playing in the standard position. Usually he used a bottleneck, or some kind of a knife or slide, and played a unison melody with the voice. He had a consistent sound to the guitar tuning, almost a sour, bitter sound, like a half ripe persimmon, and by the standards of most guitarists he was out of tune, although it may have been the sound he was trying to get. The accompaniment style was only half formed, and may reflect the different streams of music that he grew up with in McComb. The unison melody played with the slide was distinctively Mississippian, but there was no rhythm in the lower strings, either a steady thumb pattern in 4/4, as in Texas, or an alternate thumb picking like many of the delta men used. He used an open tuning, but instead of the cross fingerings or alternate chord patterns that singers like Skip James or Son House developed, he fell back on the barred subdominant. On some of the pieces derived from white sources he even tried to find fingerings for the conventional V and VI chords. On blues like ''Yellow Dog Blues'' and ''Slow Mama Slow,'' however, the guitar style was more effective, and there was an excitement even in the rhythmic irregularity. He moved freely over the guitar fingerboard between the vocal lines, some-times with a melodic figure played with the knife on the upper, middle, and bass strings. His irregularity in rhythmic structure was still closely related to the basic Mississippi style, and he used the half measure anacrusis for the vocal phrase and the extended guitar bridge between the lines. There was almost an ornate quality to his vocal melo-dies with their elaborately developed inner rhythms. There was some of the green twisting and bending of levee trees in the wind in the shifting accents of his voice in a piece like ''Signifying Blues.''

Example 19

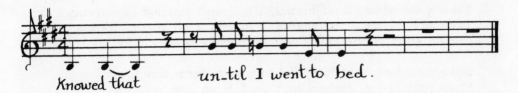

Most of his pieces were in the gapped pentatonic scale of the Mississippi blues, but the scale in "Signifying Blues" had an interesting use of the seventh tone of the scale, the d in measure 12. It seems to have functioned as the third of the chord on the dominant b, rather than a distinct scale tone, but it was one of the few songs from the early Mississippi music that used the seventh as a melodic tone. The guitar accompaniment for "Signifying" was also unusual for Collins. The pattern was an almost unvarying ostinato, similar in some ways to the kind of finger patterns that were used by the Alabama singer Ed Bell. The accompaniment was in open E tuning, with the harmonic changes only suggested in the bass strings. The text of the blues was vague, but the first verse included the unusual sexual reference to impotence, and the other verses were concerned with the "signifying" man.

> My mama signify that my black snake was dead,
> My mama signify my black snake was dead,
> But she never knowed that until I went to bed.

> I'm goin' tell everybody what a signifying man will do.
> I'm goin' tell everybody what a signifying man will do.
> He will come to my house and he'll talk about you,
>   Go to your house and he'll talk about me,
> But he better mind he ain't goin' signify no more.

> Lord, he's a signifying man, I'll tell you what it's all about.
> He's a signifying man, I'll tell you what it's all about.
> She looked down the street and seen me coming,
>   she put that low down (rascal) out.

> I'm going to tell you what you ought to do.
> I'm going to tell you what you ought to do.
> If you don't believe me you can ask everybody in my neighborhood.

One of his finest blues, "Slow Mama Slow," juxtaposed two blues themes in its four verses, an unashamed sexual enjoyment in the first and third verses, and the "leaving" theme in the second and fourth. They would have been more clearly related if Collins had altered the order to begin with the third, then described the sexual enjoyment of the first and left with the second and fourth; but he chose to leave them with their inter-relationship not immediately clear, so the verses gave to each other a stronger emotional tension by their only half sensed involvement.

125

Take your time, kind mama, I'm gonna do just as slow as I can.
Take your time, kind mama, I'm gonna go just as slow as I can.
I might start shimmyin', don't let nobody hear.

Make your bed up higher, and turn your lamp way low.
Make your bed up higher, turn your lamp way low.
I'm gonna hug and kiss you, ain't coming here no more.

Pull down your window, lock up on your door.
Lock up on your window, lock up on your door.
I got ways like the devil, I'm slipping on the floor.

Make your bed up higher, and turn your lamp around.
Make your bed up higher, turn your lamp around.
Look out your back door, see me leave this town.

By asking the woman to ''make your bed up higher,'' to make it more difficult for someone else to join her in bed, he extended the sexual theme through the song, and the blues had a vivid immediacy even though its levels of meaning were unclear. Although Collins was not one of the stylistic innovators within the Mississippi blues idiom he was enough part of it that in blues like ''Signifying Blues'' and ''Slow Mama Slow,'' he had some of the intensity of the Mississippi music at its most creative level.

In the winter of 1932 King Solomon Hill, a singer with strong similarities to Collins' singing style, recorded six titles for Paramount in Grafton, Wisconsin. The songs done by Hill were ''Whoopee Blues,'' ''Down On My Bended Knee,'' ''The Dead Gone Train,'' ''Tell Me Baby,'' ''My Buddy Blind Papa Lemon,'' and ''Times Has Done Got Out Of Hand.'' For several years Big Joe Williams, who grew up in Crawford, Mississippi, a few miles from the Alabama state line in the center of the state, claimed that he had done them using a different name and singing in a falsetto to disguise his voice. There were so many differences between these recordings and Williams' pieces done in the same period that it has been difficult to accept them as his, even with a high falsetto. They were, however, so strongly similar to Collins that there have been suggestions that Hill was Collins using a pseudonym to avoid trouble with the American Recording Corporation. Collins had recorded twenty titles for A.R.C. in October, 1931, and if he were to do any work for Paramount he would have to use a pseudonym. Despite the closeness of the vocal style, however, they seem to be separate singers. Dean Wardlow has been told that Hill was also from McComb, and may still be living there. One of Hill's pieces was about Lemon Jefferson, who was from Texas, even though he'd traveled through Mississippi before his death in 1930. So it could be that Hill was from Texas, and the similarities between his style and Collins' were only coincidental. Both of them sang in a high falsetto, with a loosely felt melodic line, but there were many differences in their musical approach, especially in the guitar accompaniments. Unlike Collins, Hill followed the voice with a drumming line in triplets in the guitar. The accompaniment, in an open D tuning, was almost entirely in single note patterns, the strings slackened so that he could get a heavy bass sound something like the lower strings of the Japanese koto.

Hill, like Garfield Akers, was a singer who had brought an individual concept to a high state of development, and his linear accompaniment style could have been a useful enlargement of the blues form. His own playing was even more effective because of his intensely dramatic approach to the music. The biting notes of the guitar were closely tied to the vocal line. He played with a slide on the upper strings and fretted the bass strings, giving him a mixture of tones something like those of Son House, who uses the metal slide as well as fretting. Also unlike Collins, Hill's falsetto was not a clear vocal sound. He sang with a mixed tone, using some head voice in the higher, forced falsetto, and he was able to sing with either a harder rasping tone or with a pure open sound. With this technical approach his voice became as effective a dramatic instrument as the guitar.

Although he used an involved compound verse for "Tell Me Baby," in "Whoopee Blues," "Down On My Bended Knee," and "The Dead Gone Train" the verse form was the usual three line stanza. His verses were not exceptional, but he persisted in an emotional attitude until it yielded some verbal richness. He had moments of self-pity in a blues like "Down On My Bended Knee,"

> At last, at last, down on my bended knee.
> At last, at last, down on my bended knee.
> I am worried about my baby, bring her back to me.

> You know I love my baby, that's why we can't get along.
> You know I love my baby, that's why we can't get along.
> Look like everything I do turns out going on wrong...

but they were in the same vein of blues poetry that has persisted from Patton's "Poor Me" to Lightning Hopkins' "A Sinner's Prayer." He was more striking in the developing imagery of a piece like "Whoopee Blues."

> Um, you been gone all day that you may make whoopee all night.
> Baby, you been gone all day that you may make whoopee all night.
> I'm going to take my razor and cut your leg off, you wouldn't
> think I been servin' you right.

> Undertaker been here and gone, I give him your height and size.
> I said undertaker been here and gone, I give him your height and size.
> You'll be making whoopee with the devil in an hour tomorrow night.

127

You done made me love you, now got me for your slave.
Baby you done made me love you, now got you for your slave.
From now on you'll be making whoopee, baby, in your lonesome
      grave.

Baby, next time you go out carry your black suit along.
Mama, next time you go out carry your black suit along.
Coffin gonna be your present, hell gonna be your brand new home.

I see the devil got 90,000 women,
      he's got me one more ....

If, like many other Mississippi singers who were once only a vague name, Hill should be found in McComb it would be an important contribution to the knowledge of the blues style in the area. If Collins and Hill were both raised in the same town, then the similarities in their vocal approach would be more easily understood. Also, if Hill should be found then he could trace some of the influences that helped shape his guitar style and its complex and dramatic involvement with the sung blues phrase.

8. CENTRAL MISSISSIPPI AND JACKSON INTO THE 'THIRTIES

The southern cities like Jackson were less isolated than the country farms and crossroads of the delta country, and there was a steady movement of professional entertainers in and out of the small night clubs and variety theatres. Most of the blues acts didn't get much below Memphis and its Lyric Theatre on Beale Street, but there were enough musicians and singers in and out of Jackson to give the town's music a self-consciousness that most of the delta singing lacked, and often the local blues men were subject to the influence of outside performers and commercial recordings. In the late years of the 'twenties, however, there was a small Jackson group centered around Ishman Bracey and Tommy Johnson that had some of the rough vigor of the freer delta music. Most of the young men in from the country hung around Johnson's house on River Front Street, but Bracey seemed to have a better business sense, and he was usually able to keep some kind of job going in Jackson.

In the early 1960's Bracey was located in Jackson by Dean Wardlow, and since that time he has been interviewed by three or four other blues enthusiasts. He is still playing, but since the late 1940's, when he joined the church, he has played only gospel songs and sacred music. He was born on January 1, 1900 near Forest Hill, not far from Jackson, and began playing when he was in his teens. His style, when he began recording in 1928, was only tentatively formed, and there was considerable variation in his performances, although some of the changes probably represented Bracey's efforts to become commercially more successful. He was perhaps most effective as a singer when he was associated with Johnson, even if Johnson's influence was only indirect. His first sessions in Memphis were probably done with Johnson as an accompaniest and they certainly reflect some of the other man's ideas. At his sessions two years later in Grafton, Wisconsin, there was almost a stylistic uncertainty to his music. Most of Bracey's compositions are still protected by copyright and permission could not be obtained to quote either melodies or texts. His earliest blues "Saturday Blues" and

129

"Left Alone Blues," recorded in February, 1928, were not copywritten, and of his early recordings they were perhaps the most important, especially "Saturday Blues," which used an interesting variation on the usual three line verse form.

There is still some question as to whether Johnson was one of the accompaniests on the record. Bracey had told Wardlow that the second guitarist was Charlie McCoy, another young Jackson musician who usually played mandolin. Johnson, however, was recording at the same time, and all three of them were in Memphis for the sessions. Ralph Peer was recording them for Victor Records. Johnson recorded on February 3 and 4, with Bracey probably playing second guitar, and Ishman did his two pieces when Johnson had finished singing. The accompaniment sound was very full on Bracey's recordings, and it could even have been all three of them. In the background one guitar was being played with a mandolin technique, a flat picked trill on a single string, and there was still a complex accompaniment pattern being played closer to the microphone.

Of all the Mississippi men Bracey was one of the few who sang with a strongly nasal tone. The sound was thin and pinched, and he sang without embellishment; even the common portmenti at the verse endings were left out. He had to depend on skillful accompaniment patterns and strong verse material to be distinctive. His verses, however, were usually derivative, and without the guitarists like Johnson, to at least shape the accompaniment, he was not a distinctive instrumentalist. In the recordings that he did for Paramount two years later, in March, 1930, he even tried using a small instrumental group for some of the pieces. It was an advertising team called the "New Orleans Nehi Boys," with clarinetist Kid Ernest Mitchell and pianist Charley Taylor. He also did two blues with his own accompaniment, "Woman Woman Blues" and "Suitcase Full Of Holes." His voice had darkened since his first recordings, and he tried to use a falsetto voice in "Woman Woman Blues," with an octave leap in the middle of the second line, but the sound was almost clumsy and the accompaniment was unsteady.

In the earlier "Saturday Blues" he used one of the conventional infidelity themes, but the form of the verses had been changed to fit a fresh melodic concept, and in one verse he loosened up enough to sing about skin powders and creams that were advertised as being able to lighten skin color.

> Now you tell me, mama, do you think that's right,
> You with your kid all day and run to me at night.
> With your kid all day and run to me at night.
> With your kid all day and run to me at night.
>
> Now my regular woman took my pocket change,
> And my sometime woman wants to do the same,
> And you better not let my people catch you here.
> Don't never let my people catch you here.

'Cause it 'tain't no tellin' she might do,
She might cut you, she might shoot you too.
Now she might cut you, she might shoot you too.
Lord she might cut you, she might shoot you too.

Now she's the meanest woman that I've ever seen,
And when I asked for water gimme gasoline.
Now ask her for water, gimme gasoline.
Lord asked for water, gimme gasoline.

Now if you want your woman to look like the race,
You buy her high brown powder, Palmer's Skin Success.
You buy her high brown powder, Palmer's Skin Success.
Buy her high brown powder, Palmer's Skin Success.

Now I got four-five puppies, got one shaggy hound,
It takes all them dogs to run my women down.
It takes all them dogs to run my women down.
Takes all them dogs to run my women down.

The harmonic structure was the usual I-IV-I-V-I, but the first line was
a loosely swinging phrase that went on to include the second line of the
verse with only a pause to take a breath. The doubled line was built
on a suspended down beat and running eighth note groups; it had some of
the feeling of a chopping song. Then there was a sudden change in the
third line to an ascending melodic figure at a tempo that seemed to slow
the opening rhythm to quarter note groups. The rising figure, repeated
in the line, almost seemed to be a structural resolution to the easy
movement of the opening phrase, bringing it up with the same motion
as a man reining in a jogging horse on a back road through the hill
country. The last line began with a half measure to open the phrase,
then resolved with an almost standard last line melody and the V-V-I-I
harmonic resolution. It was casually done, but it was a fresh working of
old blues material, and it was musically successful.

Example 20

131

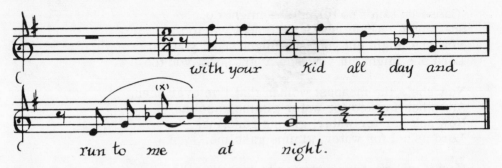

with your Kid all day and run to me at night.

Bracey, at this time, has no plans to play outside of Jackson, and he is still giving much of his time to the church. For him it has been many years since the blues were a deep influence on his life.

Most of the delta singers drifted in and out of Jackson during the 'twenties - certainly Charley Patton, Son House, Willie Brown, and Skip James, at one time or another - but the strongest influence on the music in the town's Negro neighborhoods, as well as on most of the young singers who hung around the town for more than a few weeks, was Tommy Johnson, who was living ".. in a big house on River Front Street," as one of his younger pupils, Shirley Griffith, remembers. Bracey has told Dean Wardlow that Johnson was born in Crystal Springs, in Copiah County, about 25 miles to the south of Jackson. Griffith, who was found by Art Rosenbaum in Indianapolis, said that Johnson was nearly fifty when he met him in Jackson in the late 'twenties, so Johnson would have been born about 1880. In the picture that was taken of him at the time of his recording sessions for Victor in 1928, however, he looks younger; so Griffith may have thought he was older than he was. He moved into Jackson about 1926 and lived there for a number of years, occasionally traveling to other Mississippi towns to sing. All of the men who encountered him during these years remember him as a near alcoholic who drank anything he could get his hands on. He finally went back to Crystal Springs and was living there at the time of his death in the mid-1950's.

It is difficult to reconcile Johnson's drunkenness and his difficult emotional life with his wife, Maggie Campbell, with the artistic poise of his singing. He was one of the most consciously artistic of all the Mississippi singers, and each one of his pieces had been worked into his fingers and his voice until it was a carefully distinct musical statement. His blues were like a piece of swamp cedar rubbed against a sleeve until it glistened. Griffith told Rosenbaum that "Tom was practically a genius on the guitar," and in discussing "Big Road Blues" as Griffith had learned it from Johnson, Rosenbaum concluded, "Unlike most blues guitarists who have a characteristic style which they freely apply to the various blues they sing, Johnson seems to have worked out a set accompaniment which fit the special character of each blues he did, and which he played pretty much the same each time. Here, the idea of walking down a road is suggested in the guitar bass line. Shirley says that Tom could stop the strings of the guitar from above when

132

playing this blues, as one would play a piano, rather than bring his left hand around the neck from the bottom in the usual way..." [1.] The bass figure in "Big Road" was one of Johnson's most widely imitated guitar patterns.

Example 21

It was strongly pianistic in style, with its close relationship to the boogie "walking bass," and it may have been because of this that Johnson would sometimes play it pressing down on the strings with his left hand, as a pianist would press down on the piano keys. Nearly every one of the young Jackson singers learned this figure of Johnson's, and even in recent years it has been recorded almost as he played it by Griffith, by K. C. Douglas, who also learned some of his style from Johnson, and by the older Meridian singer Babe Stovall, who was in and out of Jackson when he was a young man. Even the Memphis medicine show performers picked it up, and Furry Lewis still uses it for several of his pieces.

All of the compositions that he recorded for Victor at his Memphis sessions in February and August of 1928 - "Cool Drink Of Water Blues," "Big Road Blues," "Bye-Bye Blues," "Maggie Campbell Blues," "Canned Heat Blues," "Lonesome Home Blues," "Louisiana Blues," and "Big Fat Mama Blues" - are still protected by copyright, and the copyright holder has denied permission to quote either the verses or the melodies. In the winter of 1929-1930 he went north with Bracey and recorded for Paramount, but none of the records have been found. Often, however, he used widely known folk verses in the pieces, and it is possible to consider his style in his reworking of these traditional materials. His voice was carefully controlled, and he was very skilled in his use of falsetto. In one of his effective uses of a local verse he gave the conventional melody a new color and dimension with falsetto leaps of a major sixth or an octave, the pitch consistently true, despite the difficulty of the voice change.

Example 22

As in most of his songs the scale was derived from the older slave scales. For this verse he used a gapped pentatonic with an altered third used as both major and minor. The second and the seventh were not included. The rhythmic movement was slow, the guitar returning to pianistic figures in the bass strings, as in "Big Road Blues." He separated the vocal phrases with the irregular half measure that was characteristic of Patton and the northern delta singers, in the two beats leading to the new phrase suggesting a subtle rhythmic impetus with the accompaniment. One of his blues, "Big Fat Mama," even used the "Moon Going Down" melody, although he played it with a different accompaniment style. One of the most moving of his pieces was the slow, brooding "Canned Heat Blues," perhaps the most lyric of his blues. The text, which was concerned with drinking Sterno, had a lingering sadness in his insistence that his alcoholism was killing him.

He was often able to rework effectively an older song with only rhythmic shifts and a subtle displacement of emphasis. The melodic changes, against a complex two-guitar accompaniment, stayed in the ear, even when the text was overly familiar.

Example 23

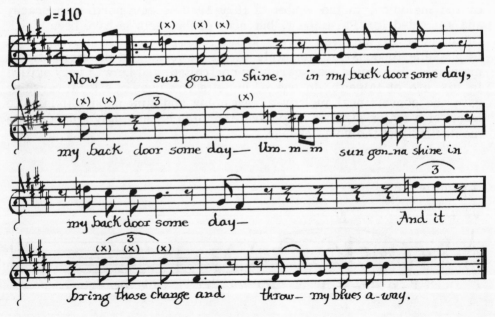

He was even able to set the "See See Rider" verse to the same melody, and the younger singers who learned it from him often slip into his melodic patterns after they've sung the traditional version. The piece was developed within the twelve bar, three line verse framework, but his changes gave it unexpected vividness. It was as though he had consciously taken the blues form apart in his mind, and then slowly put it together again. Often he seemed to be using older verses to make his melodic and rhythmic concept more immediately obvious, but it may have been that his use of the traditional verses reflected a creative impulse that was more concerned with the musical than the textual. He seemed to have few of the torments of Son House or Robert Johnson, and he didn't concern himself with the local scene in the way that Patton did. But in his use of the voice and in his accompaniments, he was as personally creative as they were, and in the blues style that was developing in central Mississippi he was deeply influential.

There was an emotional loneliness in the music of the delta singers, the feeling of the long dusty roads through the fields, and the winter sundowns around the thin board cabins when the sun turns the water blood red as it drops below the low line of the horizon. But life in the delta towns was crowded and noisy, and the music for the road houses and the dances had some of this easy gregariousness. It wasn't intense, it wasn't individual, but it was good for the long hours when people just wanted to dance and drink some illegal whiskey. It was the kind of music that went into the juke boxes when the first roadside clubs began putting in brightly lit music machines instead of hiring a local band. The bands could play almost anything, for both white and colored audiences, and the ramshackle buildings would shake with the feet stamping on the board floors as the fiddle and guitar picked up the old country dance pieces. Outside there would be a few dogs lying in the light waiting for somebody to come out and get them back across the fields with a lantern. Over the door were clouds of insects whirling around the bright light bulb that glared on the hand painted sign advertising the building. There were little breakdown bands everywhere in the South, some of them in Memphis using a jug for a comedy effect, but most of them just a fiddle and a guitar, sometimes two guitars or a mandolin, or a washboard and a kazoo. Everybody sang in the band and they usually had to know a lot of numbers to get through the dances. There was none of the creative excitement of the great delta blues in the breakdown music; the bands were like the weeds left to grow in the shade of summer corn, but just as in the fields there were sometimes more weeds than anything else.

The bands, and the men involved with them, had considerable popularity even in Mississippi, with its strong blues orientation. They didn't present the emotional challenge of someone like Willie Brown or Sam Collins, and the music was often old-fashioned, so that everybody could dance to it. A small group of central Mississippi musicians, Charlie McCoy, his brother Joe, the Chatmon brothers, and two Jackson musicians, James Cole and Tommie Bradley, did more recording than all of the delta blues men together, and they continued to work through the 1930's, when the delta style had been momentarily eclipsed by newer sounds in the blues. There was considerable overlapping of musicians between the Chatmons and the McCoys, so that the records often have a similarity of sound. Also, Cole and Bradley both sang or used outside vocalists, so their recordings lacked a strong individuality. But all of them seem to have had some sales since there were many sessions for all of them. The Mississippi Sheiks, usually Bo Chatmon and a violinist, had some releases that were very successful within their market, and occasionally there was some interest in one of the records in one of the northern Negro slums.

The groups all had a similar musical approach, not greatly different from the style of one of the Memphis jug groups, Jack Kelly's South Memphis Jug Band. The rhythm was a heavy 4/4, steady, even monotonous, but clearly defined so that there would be no difficulty dancing to it. At times the rhythms - especially when Bo Chatmon was the guitarist - were so dull that the bands were almost as bad as the white music that was being played in the area. The violinists, Lonnie Chatmon and Walter Vincon with Charlie McCoy's Mississippi Hot Footers and the Sheiks, James Cole with the Cole and Bradley groups, usually played in unison with the voice, and on instrumental breaks played the melody without variation. The accompaniment guitar style was often a flat picked alternate bass note - chord pattern similar to the standard white country style. On the Cole and Bradley recordings there was often some excitement in Eddie Dimmit's mandolin playing and in the still unidentified washboard player's busy style. Since the rhythm was already so steady they were left to buzz around it like bees around a jam pot left outside on a table. With the Sheiks there were usually only Chatmon and the violinist Walter Vincon, and the sound was less colorful; but one of their first recordings, "Sitting On Top Of The World" and "Lonely One In This Town," sold very well and many other country musicians, white and Negro, learned to play it.

Although Charlie McCoy usually played the mandolin there was a heavier sound on the Mud Steppers' recordings, as though he were playing a banjo-mandolin, with the mandolin finger board and a skin banjo head. On their version of "It Is So Good," he played rhythm chords behind some of the singing and the sound was very much like that of a banjo.

The blues that all of them did had a derivative quality, but sometimes there were moments of brilliance. For his "That Lonesome Train Took My Baby Away" McCoy had developed a fast, raggy mandolin accompaniment, and the blues was an effective elaboration of one of the standard "leaving" themes, even though his singing had an amateurish quality. The piece would have gotten everybody out on a dance floor for a noisy minute of loose-legged movement. The song had some of the feeling of a delta blues in the text, even though the music was closer to country ragtime.

> Woke up this morning, found something wrong,
> My loving babe had caught that train and gone.
> Now won't you starch my jumper, iron my overalls.
> I'm going to ride that train that they call the Cannonball.
>
> Depot agent, close your depot down.
> The woman I'm loving she's fixin' to blow this town.
> Now that mean old fireman, the cruel old engineer.
> Gonna take my baby and leave me lonesome here.
>
> It ain't no telling what that train won't do.
> It'll take your baby and run right over you.
> Now that engineer man ought to be 'shamed of hisself,
> Take women from their husbands, babies from their
>   mothers' breasts.
>
> I walked down the track and the stars refuse to shine.
> Looked every minute I was going to lose my mind.
> Now my knees was weak, my footsteps was all awry,
> Looked like every minute I was stumbling (under the way.)

Although the melody had been slightly changed by the hurried tempo, it was essentially the same as the "Saturday Blues" melody that Ishman Bracey had recorded three years earlier; so it must have been widespread in the central Mississippi area. Tommie Bradley used the same leaving theme for the opening verses of the "Window Pane Blues," with Cole's violin and Dimmitt's busy mandolin.

> Lord, when I got up this morning snow was on my window pane.
> I got up this morning, snow was on my window pane.
> I couldn't even see my baby, couldn't even hear her name.
>
> Lord and my baby is leaving, crying won't make her stay.
> My baby's leaving, crying won't make her stay.
> Lord if crying would help now, cry myself away....

One of the wildest and most exciting of the Mississippi "juking" bands was a three piece group with piano, guitar, tambourine, and sometimes a doubling on kazoo - probably by the tambourine player - that was recorded in Hattiesburg by A.R.C. in the summer of 1936. The group was called the Mississippi Jook Band, and probably included the blues singer Blind Roosevelt Graves, his brother Uaroy, and a piano player named Cooney Vaughn. Graves and his brother had recorded both blues and gospel songs for Paramount in the late 1920's, but the four sides that were released by A.R.C, "Hittin' The Bottle Stomp," "Skippy Whippy," "Dangerous Woman," and "Barbecue Bust," were closer to the rougher country barrelhouse tradition than they were to the blues. Vaughn had an uninhibited country rag time style, and the little band moved with an exuberant, strutting sound.

All of the bands could do Mississippi blues pieces. The Sheiks did a version of Tommy Johnson's "Big Road Blues" called "Stop And Listen Blues," and on other recordings there were local blues verses and melodies. Often they were recording for the white hillbilly market, rather than the blues market. Bo and his brother Sam were able to get almost a country and western purity in their singing, and pieces like "Jail Bird Love Song," sung as a duet, were very effective in their imitation of the white rural singing and accompaniment style. Bo, under the name Bo Carter, also had considerable success as a soloist, and recorded more than a hundred titles between 1928 and 1940. He had developed a musical idiom with some of the immediacy of blues artists like Lonnie Johnson and Tampa Red, and, like the Sheiks, was able to reach both a white and Negro audience. For some of his recordings he used the erotic symbolism that had become popular in the "party record" business, and he seems to have been sold to the white market on this basis. He had other pieces - "Be My Salty Dog," with its momentary similarities to John Hurt's "Candy Man," and his first songs for OKeh, "I'm An Old Bumble Bee," taken from Memphis Minnie's Columbia recording, which had been released a few months earlier, and "I've Got The Whole World In My Hand" - which, although they were not strongly individual were sung with some feeling and taste. He is still living in Memphis, blind and unable to play, his wife asking people to leave him alone so that he can think about the life to come instead of the blues. Their house is a shabby wooden building on the same rutted alleyway behind Beale Street where Will Shade of the Memphis Jug Band lives in helpless squalor.

By the middle of the 'thirties, as the Depression deepened, the delta music began to change, the concept of the blues as song shifting to a more assertive, a more obvious expression. In the new stylistic emphasis there was less concern with the complex musicianship that had led to guitar accompaniments like Willie Brown's "Future Blues" or the beautifully ordered melodies like Tommy Johnson's "Cool Drink of Water Blues." Instead there was a heightened emotionalism, a new intentness. It was the same urgency that dominated Patton's music, but the rhythms had been subtly altered to suit new dancing styles and a new city audience. One of the first Mississippi men to record extensively in the developing style was Joe Williams, who was in his thirties and living in St. Louis when he began recording in 1935. He was born in Crawford, Mississippi, in Lowndes County, about seventy miles north of Meridian. Like Sam Collins, he grew up out of the delta counties, and this was a shaping factor in his musical development. He was one of sixteen children, and he decided when he was still young that he didn't want to stay in the fields as a laborer. He made his own guitar when he was four and a half, and by the time he was in his teens he was already writing blues. For most of the 'twenties he was drifitng around the South, working in levee camps or in the line camps in the back country, playing music for dances and parties. For two or three years he lived in Tuscaloosa, Alabama, working at parties for a local pimp named Totsie King. Finally, in the worst of the Depression, he made his way to St. Louis and settled down. His cousin J. D. Short, who had recorded for Paramount and Vocalion, had been living in St. Louis since 1925, and he and Joe worked around St. Louis together until J. D. began playing saxophone and clarinet with Douglas Williams' dance band. When Joe went to Chicago to record for Bluebird in February, 1935, his second guitarist was Henry Townsend.

With Williams, and with other singers who developed in the late 'thirties and in the war years, the manner of singing became, in itself, the style of the song. He used every kind of blues from Mississippi, as well as pieces he learned from the recordings of men like Sleepy John Estes, and he performed everything with the same shouted ferocity. His "Someday Baby," from Estes' older recording of "Someday Baby Blues," had some of the feeling of Estes loose, jangling rhythm, but Williams sang it with the rough intensity of his own "Baby Please Don't Go," or his "Highway 49." His accompaniment style was a strummed rhythm using dotted note values in an almost loping beat, and insistent, knotted passages of running triplets. Musically the accompaniments were tangled and often confused, but like his voice, it was the expressiveness of the performance that shaped the blues, rather than the musical concept of the piece shaping the performance, as with singers like Tommy Johnson or King Solomon Hill. For his second session in 1935, he began using a larger instrumental group, and on many of his later Bluebird recordings between 1937 and 1941, the sound was closer to the small bands working in the Jackson area than it was to the spare delta accompaniments. The harmonica player Sonny Boy Williamson worked with him for a number of recordings, and Sonny Boy's playing was as emotionally driven as Williams' singing.

Although it was his style of performance rather than his compositions that gave him his distinctiveness, he had considerable variety in his recordings. One of the most interesting of the early Bluebird releases was a fine "My Grey Pony," with some similarities to Patton's style in "Pony Blues," but with a distinctive accompaniment and phrase pattern. "I'm Getting Wild About Her" even used an easy, rolling version of the "Tight Like That" melody. When he began recording as a "folk" blues artist in the 1950's he reworked his old material over and over again, often using phrases and patterns of the guitar accompaniments with a new urgency, and sometimes singing with an even more intense drama. His voice had deepened in the years that he had been away from recording, and his style had become even more knotted in its use of forms and techniques, both from his own background and from other recordings. Some of the individuality of the sound was from his use of altered nine-string guitars. He used old instruments and mounted an additional set of three tuning pegs at the end of the neck. The strings were tuned in unison with the two high strings of the guitar and with the third string of the bass, leaving the two low bass strings and the third string from the top of the instrument as single melody strings. Most of the pieces used the "Spanish" open G tuning, which on Joe's instrument was d-g-d'-d'-g'-b-b-d''-d'', and he alternated a finger stroke on the open strings with heavy melodic passages on the middle strings, usually with a knife or metal slide. For most of his pieces the guitar was played in unison with the voice, although as he became excited the guitar often was left silent while he sang. On the faster pieces, using either a compound verse form or a version of the old "Tight Like That" melody, he stayed with a mixed dotted rhythm and triplet beat pattern, usually accelerating considerably during the song. For most of his blues he used one of his older melodies, accompanying all of them with the same impetuous strength. The phrase length varied considerably in all of his performances, although he sometime was held to a more regular twelve bar pattern by his accompanists. He is still, after nearly forty years of singing, a complex and often effective performer, and his style still is moving toward an even deeper maturity.

The same emotionalism marked the singing of younger men like Robert Johnson, and of less well known delta men who were momentarily drawn into the stream of Mississippi recording in the 'thirties, like Isaiah Nettles - "The Mississippi Moaner," George Torey, and Willie Lofton. Nettles, who recorded in Jackson in 1935, used the falsetto voice and the clearly outlined melody of the older delta blues; but in his "It's Cold In China Blues," the emotionalism of the voice was forced, and the guitar rhythm was close to Big Joe's doubled strumming, almost like a "shake dance" rhythm in its noisy enthusiasm. Torey was one of the singers recorded in Birmingham by the American Recording Corporation in the summer of 1937, but his style had many of the delta characteristics. Older Mississippi singers have vaguely remembered him as being from one of the northern delta counties. Of the three sides by Torey listed in the Dixon and Godrich compilation, one - unissued - was titled "Delta Blues," which strengthens the impression that he was probably a Mississippi man who was either living in Birmingham or who had been brought into town for the session. His other two pieces, "Married Woman Blues" and "Lonesome Man Blues," also recorded on April 2, were released on ARC 7-08-57. His voice had some of Williams' assertive strength, with a consistent vibrato on the held tones and even a dramatic use of dynamic shading. The guitar accompaniment for "Lonesome Man Blues" was in a more controlled bottleneck style, with a steady rhythm in the lower strings - alternating thumb on the chord fundamental and the chord in the middle strings - and a near unison melody with the voice. The rhythm was held even through the fairly elaborate guitar interpolations played with the bottleneck between the vocal phrases. "Married Woman Blues" was more derivative in melody and accompaniment style, with some of the elements of the "raggy" guitar music that the Carolina men like Blind Boy Fuller were recording. The melody was the eight bar blues phrase probably best known in its "Keys To The Highway" version. The harmonic pattern is I - V - IV - IV - I - V - I - I, and it is usually played at a medium tempo. Torey finger picked the accompaniment, without the bottleneck, and some of his finger patterns were very reminiscent of Fuller. The verses, as with "Lonesome Man Blues," were derivative, but he used some of the most effective verses with this theme,

If you love a married woman you gonna always have the blues.
Everytime you want to see her her husband want to see her too...

and he ended with the poignant blues image,

Well, I went to the window and I looked down on that ground,
And my heart struck sorrow and the tears come easing down.

The strident emotionalism was even more evident in a blues like Willie Lofton's "Dark Road Blues." It was Tommy Johnson's old "Big Road Blues," but by 1935, when Lofton recorded for Bluebird in Chicago, it had become the more expressive "dark road" that the singer was going down. The new version had most of the elements of Johnson's accompaniment in the ascending bass line and the displaced rhythmic accent, but Lofton sang it almost twice as fast as Johnson, and the guitar playing had a hardness and an aggressiveness that Johnson would not have recognized.

By the late 'thirties the rough, shouted blues had become almost a mannerism, and some Mississippi singers developed a style that was even more intense than Williams'. One of the most successful was Tommy McClennan, who was born in April, 1908 on a farm owned by J. F. Sligh, about nine miles outside of Yazoo City. Yazoo City is in Yazoo County, about forty-five miles north of Jackson on the Clarksdale Road. He was already playing when he was in his teens and people in Yazoo City still remember his version of the juking song "Bottle It Up And Go." He was living on Charles Street in Jackson during much of the period when he was recording, a small thin, nervous man who drank heavily. He did a "Whiskey Head Woman" on his first Bluebird session in 1939, and it was successful enough for him to follow it with a "Whiskey Head Man" the next year. Not only had the blues become consciously rough and assertive, but in McClennan there was a self-conscious glorification of his own roughness. He introduced it with,

This is Tommy McClennan, the one who put the "Whiskey Headed Woman Blues." Instead of putting out the "Whiskey Headed Woman Blues" I'm going to put out "He's A Whiskey Headed Man Blues," just like myself and all the rest of you Whiskey Headed Men.

There had always been a consciousness of the drunkenness and the amorality of the life that many of the bluesmen lived, but McClennan used it as the shaping force in his blues style. His singing was often a toneless shout, a harsh, almost formless vocal line with sudden moments of excitement or laughter. His guitar playing was limited to heavy frailing in an open tuning, the intervals between the sung phrases filled with repeated single notes high on the guitar neck, or abrupt, hurried open chords. He probably used one of the metal bodied guitars that had become popular in the delta for its louder sound. McClennan's style would probably have been less effective without his rich exuberance and noisy vanity. The shouted boast in one of his blues, "I'm a guitar king, playin' the blues everywhere I go..." was somehow appealing when it was made by someone who played the guitar as badly as McClennan did.

With McClennan the assertiveness was more than a mannerism. He was noisy and vain and difficult to control. Bill Broonzy remembered that when McClennan first came to Chicago he was singing a piece that used the word "nigger," and he refused to change the word despite Bill's pleas. They went to a party together, Tommy insisting, "The hell with them. I'll sing my song..." and he went ahead and sang it. His guitar was smashed in the fight that broke out and he and Bill had to run to get away from the crowd. When he died in the late 1950's he was a hopeless alcoholic drifting on the streets of Chicago's south side.

McClennan's records sold fairly well, and another singer, Robert Petway, whose style was very similar to his, also had some of his success recording for Bluebird in 1941 and 1942. His beat was heavier and more regular, but the rest of the style - the coarse shout of the vocal line and the fierce assertiveness - was very close to McClennan's. The blues that he did at his two sessions were mostly conventional pieces of the late '30's early '40's, but occasional verses were marked with the stronger emotionalism of the delta music.

ALABAMA

9. ALABAMA

Along U. S. 43, from Mobile on the coast, through Tuscaloosa in the middle of the state, to Florence, not far from the Tennessee line, Alabama is like three different pieces of earth, the edges only loosely joined together as the road moves north through the state. Along the coast, and for almost a hundred miles inland, the land is a sandy plain covered with an endless growth of longleaf pine, rising into small ridges as the land from the rocky coastal shelf breaks through the low plain. It is empty, barren country, the cabins in scattered clearings, the nights dark and unfriendly, the days hot and oppressive. The people of Mobile still have some of the casualness of Louisiana French-Italian country, but in the pine barrens the stillness is a presence hanging in the wind, and the life in the lonely cabins is meager and thin. The pine barrens open out to the north and the land turns darker, to the rich, flat soils of the central Alabama "black belt," its name partly from the color of the dirt and partly from the thousands of Negroes who found themselves living there as "freedmen" at the end of the Civil War. The black belt, almost a hundred miles of it, reaches north of Tuscaloosa, and because of the soil was for many years one of the world's richest cotton areas, despite the debilitating methods of agriculture that were used on the land in the first years of planting. The cash value of the cotton crop was so high that during the slavery period the cotton planters didn't even grow food. They used every acre of the land for cotton and brought their food in from the coastal lands, where the small farmers could get in two or three plantings of corn and beans a year. North of Tuscaloosa the land begins to rise, and the north of the state is hill country, the roads streaked with sticky red clay and the board cabins off the highway in the new growth of loblolly and shortleaf pine, oak and sweetgum.

Culturally the state is divided like its land. Along the coast there is a French creole flavor to the language and customs. South of Mobile, in the bayous, there is as much French spoken as there is in the Louisiana bayous to the west. In Julian Lee Rayford's colorful study of the

147

Alabama bayou folk culture, "Whistling Woman and Crowing Hen," he found that the people, the speech, and the bayous have mingled into a cultural entity that is no longer French, not yet American, but with an insistent vitality in its moods and tempers. In the black belt African and American elements mingle in the Negro country areas, with the American popular culture strongest in the towns. North of the cotton country, in the hills, the culture becomes Anglo-American. Many of the early settlers were Tories who moved into the new Alabama territory rather than join the revolution, and English ballads and dance songs can still be found on the small farms back in the valleys around Huntsville and Athens. The people who came into Alabama brought their language and song with them, like the cotton seed and the fruit tree cuttings that they had packed into their wagons and saddle bags.

There were as many factors that could have led to a vital blues growth in Alabama as there were in Mississippi. The cotton lands were cleared with slave labor in the 1820's, and at the outbreak of the Civil War the population of the state was nearly half Negro. By 1880 it was still more than forty-seven percent colored, and even in 1950, after three generations of Negro families had begun to move away from the state's vicious social system, there were still more than thirty-two percent colored in Alabama. Most of the people were on farms or in isolated cabins. In 1960 only forty-five percent of the state's people had moved into the urban areas around Mobile, Gadsden, Montgomery, Huntsville, and Birmingham. It is poor country, the rate of growth much below that of the rest of the United States, and the colored men and women in Alabama live outside of the state's white social structure in almost as much isolation as the Negroes of the delta. There is a strong voodoo cult centered in the south of the state and extending up the Tombigbee River, and in the Taladega National Forest there are small groups still using African words and phrases in their speech. One of the few early song collections that included blues verses was done in Alabama, outside of Auburn in Lee County in 1904. But if there was a strong early blues tradition it has been blown into the wind, like cotton lint along the roadsides. There was little recording of Alabama artists away from the state, and there was almost no recording done in Alabama until the Gennett Record Company set up a studio in Birmingham in the summer of 1927. They left after getting some local jazz bands, a few religious groups, and a handful of blues releases. A few recordings done in Atlanta by Columbia Records and a session in Chicago for Paramount by one of the Alabama singers, with a few scattered songs by local artists, are the only pieces left of what might have been a strong indigenous blues style.

Birmingham itself may have discouraged the record companies. It's a dreary, shabby city with rows of ramshackle Negro shacks just south of the main business section. Even along the one or two streets where there are a few Negro businesses the colored men and women have a guarded nervousness if they have to talk to someone who is white. The local men working as talent scouts in other large southern cities brought most of the blues singers to the companies, but there

148

doesn't seem to have been anyone working in Birmingham. The music that was recorded, however, doesn't have the urgency or the emotional excitement of the Mississippi blues, and extensive field recording in the state in the late 1930's, the 1940's, and the early 1950's, did not yield either important blues singers or the remnants of a major strain of blues expression. A social background can only shape artistic expression if the expression is already part of the social environment. Whatever the reason there does not seem to have been the eddying stream of the blues that flooded over the flat lands of the Mississippi delta. Even the Alabama work song was less developed in its forms than the work song of Mississippi. There is only a handful of early examples, but in almost all of them the form is a one line phrase, musically complete, without the rhymed second line that was probably at the root of the blues growth in Mississippi. Without a formed verse pattern, however rudimentary, the development of the blues is severely restricted, and it could have been this lack of a verse form in the work song that inhibited the development of a local blues tradition.

Although the blues strains in Alabama seem to have been thin, the state has a rich musical culture. After a long session of blues and play party songs with a singer from the Selma area, west of Montgomery, his wife asked if she could sing. For an hour she and her sister improvised two voice religious songs with a depth and urgency that her husband's blues had never reached. The strongest song styles in Alabama are religious, and the surge song and the slow two-voice antiphonal hymn have perhaps reached their highest development in the field cabins along the Tombigbee River, or in the older settlements in the red clay country of Fayette or Marion counties.

The Alabama singers who did record, however, were distinctive. Their music was as much an expression of the black belt counties as the Mississippi singing was of the delta. Only two singers seem to have recorded extensively, Ed Bell, and a singer known only as "Barefoot Bill From Alabama," but their style was fully formed, and it is possible to see its outlines in their recordings. Barefoot Bill also worked with another singer, Pillie Bolling, on his 1930 Atlanta sessions, but Bolling had a vocal sound closer to the Georgia singers than to the Alabama, and he may have been an Atlanta man. The singing of Bell and Barefoot Bill was less intense than the Mississippi style, but it was freer rhythmically than most of the delta singing. There was the same use of the half measure for the opening phrase of a line, but the irregular shouted tone of the field song was kept, often forcing the singers into measures of 6/4 in a basic 4/4 pattern. As in Mississippi the scales were generally pentatonic. The relative restraint of the early Alabama men may have been a characteristic of the local blues styles, and the later field recordings in the state are marked with a controlled emotionalism. There also seems to have been less use of the falsetto voice that was common in Mississippi. One of the most distinctive sounds of early Alabama music was the voice of Jaybird Coleman, a harmonica

player player and singer from Bessemer, in Jefferson County, about thirteen miles southwest of Birmingham. He followed the melodic phrase of the harmonica with his voice, and he strained his voice with a tight, quivering sound to get up into the harmonica's higher range, instead of using the less difficult falsetto.

The guitar accompaniments also differed considerably from the Mississippi styles. There was almost no use of the guitar to follow the vocal melody, either with a unison melody picked with the fingers on the upper strings or with a bottle neck or metal slide. Instead there was a lighter doubled rhythm in 8th notes, the thumb hitting the fundamental of the chord and the first finger brushing back on the strings. The lines of the vocal melody were usually followed by a repeated short phrase in the guitar, generally a measure in length. The guitar style was closer to the African music of the stringed lyres or the sansa, sometimes even repeating a simple syncopated rhythmic unit throughout the piece. There was in some of it the sound of the West Indian meringue style, which was also closely involved with earlier African music, especially in its syncopated rhythm, which was less prevalent in the more isolated delta area. It was a style that could have come into Alabama through the port of Mobile, with its ships going to and from the ports of the Caribbean.

The verse forms were generally the conventional three line stanza, sometimes with the beginning line on a subdominant harmony. Barefoot Bill used a more involved verse form for two or three of his pieces.

> My baby quit me, talk's all over,
>   I said, town,
> My baby done quit me, talk's all over town.
> And I'm too good a man for to let that talk go 'round

> (Squabblin' Blues)

Many of the verses were obviously derived from city recordings, but others more directly reflected the squalor of share cropper life in Alabama. In 1963 a field collector for the Newport Folk Foundation, Ralph Rinzler, found an elderly singer named Willie Doss living in Ashford, Alabama, in the southeast corner of the state. Willie was born in Cleveland, Mississippi, and spent his boyhood there, but his singing has the characteristic Alabama softness, and he uses the Alabama 8th note rhythms, without melodic doubling, in his simple guitar accompaniments. He learned many of his songs from recent commercial recordings, but in one of his pieces he used verses that could be a survival of a disguised "escape" song from the slavery period.

> Well, I got a coal black mare, oh lord how that horse can run.
> Yes, she run out on the track at midnight, and she runs
>   all on the road.

151

ED BELL ADVERTISEMENT

Yes, she on the race track at midnight,
'Til she runs both night and day.
Say when day began to break, boys,
She don't never break her gait.

She got pretty gold teeth, earrings in her ears.
She got pretty gold teeth, earrings in her ears.
Yes when you win the race boys, you don't know how it's done.

Well she runs every night
'Til she runs to the break of day.
'Til she runs 'til she runs both night and day.
Yeh when day began to break, boys, she don't never break her
    gait.

The sensed violence was more open in the blues of Barefoot Bill.

Now Mister, Mister, please to spare my,
    I say, life,
Now Mister, Mister, please to spare my life.
I got three little children, I got one little bald headed wife.

(Squabblin' Blues)

My crime, my crime I really can't under -
    I said, stand.
My crime, my crime I really can't understand.
They got me 'cused of murder and I never harmed a man.

Baby, please come down there for my trial.
I said, babe, will you please come down on the trial day.
When my grief comes down you can wipe my tears away.

I'm going to be condemned early tomorrow,
    I said, morn,
Buddy, he condemned early on tomorrow morn.
But I'm not guilty 'cause I done nobody wrong...

(My Crime Blues)

In Bell there was the restlessness and the gnawing loneliness of the
southern itinerant.

Two trains running, never one my way.
Two trains running, never one my way.
I'm going to leave here walkin' on the Santa Fe.

Well, there's one thing I don't like 'bout that railroad man.
One thing I don't like 'bout that railroad man.
They will take your rider never bring her back.

(Frisco Whistle Blues)

153

That same train, that same engineer,
That same train, that same engineer,
Took my woman, lord, left me standing here...

Hey Mr. Conductor, can a broke man ride your blinds?
Hey Mr. Conductor, can a broke man ride your blinds?
Said "Better buy your ticket, know this train ain't mine."

I stood here looked at the risin' sun.
I was standin' lookin' at the risin' sun.
Train don't run by be some walkin' done.

(Mean Conductor Blues)

Of the two Bell's blues sound closer to the earlier work song style, but his blues include references to railroads like the Frisco or the Santa Fe, which may indicate that he learned them from other singers, since these railroads didn't go through Alabama. Despite lengthy trips through the state, nothing is known either of Ed Bell or Barefoot Bill. Jaybird Coleman has died, but everyone in Bessemer remembered him and said to talk to his brother, Joe Coleman, who shines shoes in a barber shop on Bessemer's main street. Joe keeps shining shoes as he talks, to avoid trouble with the owner of the shop, but he talks about Jaybird as he works, shaking his head from time to time saying, "I sure would like to get one of Jaybird's old records so I could hear him again. He could make that harp talk."

A last factor inhibiting the growth of the blues in the state may have been Alabama's poverty. With the coming of the boll weevil in 1910 the state's already uncertain economic growth was slowed, and despite the recent development of a large missile and electronics complex around Huntsville, the rural areas are still fast in the grip of poverty and prejudice. More than 200,000 Negroes fled the state between 1950 and 1960, and as they found rooms and apartments in the slums of Chicago and Los Angeles, they were followed by thousands of white Alabamians who had also fled the poverty and the sense of economic helplessness. With them has gone much of the elusive sound of the Alabama blues, and only an occasional note or guitar pattern, drifting in a half-open hotel room window near Schuster's Alley in Montgomery, or across a wooden porch on one of the dirt streets behind Davis Avenue in Mobile, still hangs in the air in the slow Alabama twilight.

10. ALABAMA INTO THE 'THIRTIES

There was relatively so much less recording in the Alabama area than there was in areas like the delta or north Texas that each of the sessions was an important one. Even Birmingham sessions, like the sides that were done by William Harris and George Torey, used Mississippi men. Except for the two blues men, Ed Bell and Barefoot Bill, most of the Alabama recording in the late 'twenties was done by groups like the Birmingham Jug Band, which did nine titles for OKeh in Atlanta in 1930. The jug band, which may have had Jaybird Coleman on harmonica, had a strong, loosely swinging beat, and their pieces had the tonal richness and the coloration of the best country jug band music. Joe Evans and Arthur McClain also recorded in Birmingham and New York as "The Two Poor Boys," doing minstrel songs and country dance pieces with some of the feeling of white country music of the area. One Alabama religious group, however, the Birmingham Jubilee Singers, between 1926 and 1930 did more recording than all of Alabama's blues men together. Of the handful of other men to record, the two harmonica players, Jaybird Coleman and Bullet Williams, emerged as among the most distinctive musicians within the loose framework of the Alabama style.

The handful of recordings that Coleman did in the late 1920's are still little known, but Jaybird himself is remembered in Birmingham and in Bessemer, a shambling town of low shacks about ten miles south of Birmingham, where he lived for a number of years. His brother was even able to find an old snapshot of him. Jaybird's real name was Burl C. Coleman and he was born in Gainesville in 1891. Joe remembered that his brother learned to play the harmonica "...on the banks of the Tombigbee River," and that there wasn't anyone like him anywhere around Gainesville, even though a lot of people were beginning to play the harmonica. Jaybird was drafted in the First World War, and got his nickname at Camp McClennan. He kept running off the post so much that they began calling him "jaybird," and the name stuck with him. During the 'twenties he became so well known that for a time he was managed by a local Klu Klux Klan group, who got him jobs at neighboring dances and parties. Joe remembers one time when he and Jaybird decided to walk the forty-two miles to Tuscaloosa, Alabama and Jaybird earned them more than ninety dollars stopping by the country cabins and asking if there were any songs that anyone wanted played. During most of this period he was living in Birmingham, and he was one of the small group of artists to record for the Electrobeam Gennett series when the company set up a portable unit in the city. Nothing that he recorded seems to have sold very well, but Gennett was related to a number of other companies and his masters were used for releases on Gennett, Black Patti, Champion, Conqueror, and Silvertone. At his first session, in July, 1927, he tried to work with a guitarist, R. D. Norwood, but their pieces were not used. Instead Jaybird returned to the studio a month later and redid his pieces, including the piece that he had sung with Norwood accompanying him. The musical style - voice, with accompanying harmonica used to follow the vocal phrase - was wide spread in the rural counties, but there were only a few recordings of these harmonica blues. Jaybird's songs were searing, impassioned statements, with the voice and the harmonica straining to answer each other in a series of freely sung work song phrases. Everything that he recorded was exciting, but perhaps the best known of his releases was "Mean Trouble Blues" and "Trunk Busted - Suitcase Full Of Holes," on Gennett 6245. "Trunk Busted" was the piece that his brother was most anxious to hear. "Mean Trouble Blues" used the single line verse form of much Alabama work song and reflected some of the formlessness and the rough phrasing of the music.

Example 24

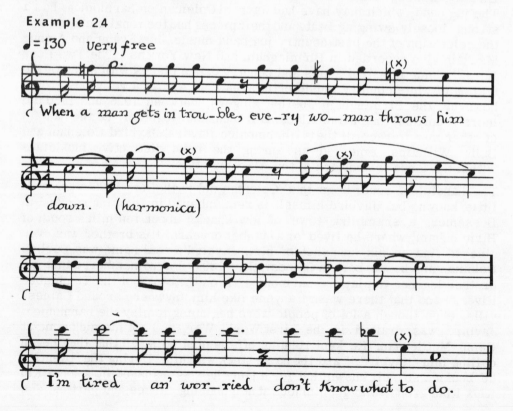

♩ = 130   Very free

When a man gets in trou-ble, eve-ry wo—man throws him

down.   (harmonica)

I'm tired   an' wor—ried   don't know what to do.

When a man gets in trouble every woman throws him down.
    (instrumental line)
I'm so worried, don't know what to do.
    (inst.)
I woke up this morning, mama, feeling sad and blue.
    (inst.)
But the woman had done quit me, didn't have nowhere to go.
    (inst.)
Hey, hi, hi, hi, hi.
    (inst.)
When I'm in my good whiskey this the way I sing my blues.
    (instrumental chorus to end)

Although there was some feeling of rhyme in the end words of the lines, blue- go - do, the other lines, down - hi, were unreleated, and the harmonica line tended to separate the piece into distinctive phrase units, rather than tying it into a related whole.

There was a last recording for Columbia in April, 1930, and Jaybird may have recorded with the Birmingham Jug Band later in the year, although it is difficult to determine the personnel of the group. Through the thirties he "toughed it out," moving to a small house on West 19th Street in Bessemer. He was almost a lone blues voice in the town, and he finally became the local "clown," with only the crying sound of his music to give away whatever he was feeling. He played a lot with the neighborhood children, and he made a living of sorts carrying a sign board for a local feed store. He stood on the crowded corners on Saturday playing his harmonica and singing, with the advertising signs hanging down his chest and back and a black derby on his head. When he became sick early in 1950 he was eligible for care in a Veteran's hospital, and it was in the Tuskeegee VA Hospital that he died on June 16, 1950.

Coleman was an intense, earthy performer, his music still a half-formed blues style. He used the blues harmonica's pentatonic scale, but his rhythmic sense extended over the long chant line, rather than a clearly measured metrical framework. He was a transitional blues figure as well as one of the most brilliant harmonica players of the 'twenties. Despite the strong elements of the past - the involved rhythm and the almost archaic scale pattern - the recordings were rich and moving as contemporary blues statements.

Like Coleman, George "Bullet" Williams played the harmonica, and there was some of the same Alabama single line verse in the recordings he did with a singer in Chicago in 1928. He could also play in a more conventional style, however, and he was the harmonica accompanist for Big Joe Williams' first recording for Vocalion in 1929. Like Jaybird, he was in some ways unable to find a way to live in the South, so he drank heavily, usually straining the cooking fuel "Sterno" through pieces of cloth for its alchoholic content. In 1934 he was working with his cousin Booker White at a roadhouse outside of West Point, Mis-

COFFEE GRINDER BLUES

**Hear JAYBIRD COLEMAN
Brag—*"No man in this town
can grind coffee like* mine!"**

Record No. 14534-D, 10 inch, 75c

COFFEE GRINDER BLUES
Man Trouble Blues } *Vocals . . .* Jaybird Coleman

Ask your dealer for the latest Race Record Catalog
Columbia Phonograph Company, 1819 Broadway, New York City

"Magic Notes"

Columbia "NEW PROCESS" **Records**
Viva-tonal Recording - The Records without Scratch

JAYBIRD COLEMAN ADVERTISEMENT

sissippi, and the next year went with Booker to Aberdeen, Mississippi. Booker remembers that Williams was from a farm not far from Selma, Alabama, and that he had begun playing while he was still living there. He would play until he passed out; then after he'd had some time to sleep it off he'd get back on the bandstand and finish the job. By the end of his life he was drinking almost anything that he could get alcohol out of, like shoe polish, as well as commercial rubbing alchohol. He seems to have lived through the 'thirties, but he is said to have died in Alabama in the 'forties. Like Coleman he was a transitional figure, but the blues that he did with an unidentified singer on Paramount 12680, "Touch Me Light Mama" and "Middlin' Blues," were more formed than Coleman's, and there was, in some of the verses, a use of almost conventional blues material.

Touch me light, pretty mama, this may be your last.
Hey, hey, this may be your last.
Touch me light, pretty mama, this may be your last.
        (spoken) Touch 'em, kid, touch 'em.

I went to the nation, then to the territore.
Couldn't find my good girl, honey, nowhere I go.
        (spoken) Touch 'em again.

Woke up this morning, woke up day before,
Woke up this morning with the same thing on my mind.
        (spoken) Touch 'em now.

I believe to my soul, mama, got to leave your town.
I ain't got no pretty mama, talk baby talk to me.
        (spoken) Touch 'em, boy, touch 'em.

Aw, talk baby talk to me.
Ain't got no pretty mama, talk baby talk to me.

I went to the nation, went back to the territore.
I couldn't find my good girl, honey, no where I go.
        (spoken) Touch 'em, touch 'em.

Honey, I believe to my soul got to leave your town,
-, got to leave your town.
        (spoken) Touch 'em, touch 'em now.

Goin' uptown, mama, talk with the chief of police.
Tell him my good girl done quit me, sure can't see no peace.

The "Touch 'em" (or "Catch 'em - the voice is difficult to under-stand) seems to be an exhortation to Williams to play the harmonica. There was a rude verse form developing from the field cry's melodic style, although in some of the verses the rhymes were irregular and forced, territore - go, and in others, town - me, not even considered.

The excitement of the performance was in the dissonant clash between the voice and the harmonica. Williams had developed a style of humming into the harmonica with a high, almost screaming sound, and the insistent instrumental line was an effective contrast with the heavy voice of the singer. The other two sides recorded by Williams for Paramount were harmonica solos, a train piece, "Frisco Leaving Birmingham," and "The Escaped Convict," both released on Paramount 12651.

It is possible that the vocalist on Williams' recordings was a young Birmingham singer named Wiley Barner, who recorded for Gennett in the summer of 1927 with piano and guitar accompaniment by Jimmy Allen and Will Jennings. There were some similarities in the sound of the voice. The vocal tone was strong and heavy, and both men sang almost without vibrato, in a flattened sound that tended to be unsteady in pitch. The singing with Williams, recorded in 1928, was closely related to the Alabama field music, however, and the Barner recordings were more conventional in their melodic structure. Despite the amateurish quality of Barner's 1927 recordings the pieces themselves were of some interest in their verse structure. In "My Gal Treats Me Mean" - released with "If You Want A Good Woman - Get One Long And Tall" on Gennett 6261 - the verse form was one of the less common blues forms that repeats the second line of the stanza rather than the first.

> Take your picture, hang it in a frame,
> When you're gone I'll see you just the same.
> When you're gone I'll see you just the same.
> When you're gone I'll see you just the same.
>
> Believe my soul my gal's got a black cat bone,
> Treat me mean and now won't let me 'lone.
> Treat me mean and I won't let her 'lone.
>
> See that spider climbin' up the wall,
> Huntin' some place to get his ashes hauled.
> Huntin' some place to get his ashes hauled.
> Well, he hunt some place to get his ashes hauled.
>
> Bring my slippers, (   ) my yard.
> Hear me tippin' toward my good gal's yard.
> Hear me tippin' toward my good gal's yard.
> You can't hear me tippin' toward my good gal's yard.

The American Recording Corporation worked in Birmingham again in 1937, and recorded a number of local artists, among them James Sherrill, who used the pianist Robert McCoy as accompaniest. Sherrill's blues, released under the pseudonym "Peanut The Kidnapper," were strongly influenced by the recordings of the popular Peetie Wheatstraw. Mack Rhineheart and Brownie Stubblefield also recorded a number of blues duets during this period, in Chicago and in Birmingham. The music, with piano and guitar accompaniment, was, like Sherrill's, derivative, and was not strongly rooted in any of the southern blues areas. The Alabama music, as it streamed into the main current of southern Negro music, merged its distinctive style with the heavier eddies of music from Mississippi, Texas, Chicago and the Atlantic seaboard.

TEXAS

11. TEXAS

There is a flatness to the Gulf Coastal Plain of Texas, a flatness and emptiness. In the oil country around Beaumont and Houston the lights on the drilling rigs light up the countryside for miles around, their lights on moonless nights like stars hanging above the dark line of the horizon. The coastline itself is a ragged marsh of drowned trees and shifting sandbars, with yellow lines of silt marking the mouths of the creeks and rivers that empty into the Gulf of Mexico. There are few roads along the edge of the water. The highways are further inland, with small dirt roads going down to the creek mouths. The blackened trees are hung with swamp moss and the air is heavy with the noise of birds and insects. In eastern Texas, from the west bank of the Sabine River that marks the boundary with Louisiana, there is a belt of southern yellow pine, still only partly cleared. The trees thin toward the west as they mingle with the scrub oak forest that covers the broad flat lands of the eastern part of the state. The earth becomes dry and sandy, the trees clustered in meandering stream beds or in the lower ground between the low, eroded hills. As the land slowly rises to the west the trees become thinner and the ground is covered with dry, bunched grass. In the cotton country, mostly within the triangle formed by Austin, Houston, and Dallas, the land rises in choppy clay hills, the back roads impassable in the spring rains and hung with choking dust in the summer heat. The land is still empty, stretching in low eddies below the drifting cover of thin clouds, rising only a few hundred feet in the long miles between the coastal swamp and the sharecropper cabins outside of Waco, more than one hundred fifty miles inland.

Driving along the roads of Texas, even in the eastern half of the state, is tiresome and monotonous through the low hills and the empty country-side. Across the grasslands and the stretches of plowed cotton fields the water towers of the small towns gleam like squat moons, and the towns themselves have a shabby similarity. Rosenburg, with its block of one story red-brick buildings and its small, sun bleached houses. Brenham, with its courthouse square and its farm supply stores with their corrugated iron roofs over the sidewalks on the back streets. Everywhere in the United States there has been a persistent drift from the countryside into the cities, and it has been even more pronounced in Texas. In 1930 forty-two percent of the state's population still lived on farms, but, after the Depression and the years of the war, in 1960 less than ten percent were still living outside of the growing cities. Along the roadsides are empty farm cabins with their crumbling walls and broken shutters swinging in the wind. In the smaller towns the older buildings are empty, the warehouses and feed stores doing a slow and intermittent business during the long days of summer. The Texas oil boom, beginning with the Spindletop Well in 1901, has brought wealth to the state, but most of the money has stayed in the cities.

There was little of the oppressive plantation life of the Mississippi delta to shape the Texas blues. It is even difficult to find a fully developed early blues style that is distinctly Texan, although there was a strong tradition of work and play songs. In some Mississippi counties the Negro population is more than eighty percent of the people living in the county, and it is only in recent years that the number of Negroes in the state has slipped to less than half of the population. At its highest point, just after the Civil War, the colored population of Texas was less than thirty percent of the state's still sparse growth. In 1880, as people moved in from other states, the state grew to a million and a half people, and only twenty-five percent were Negroes. By 1950 the percentage of Negro to white in the state had dropped to about twelve percent. Even the farm system which had kept most southern Negroes in economic servitude after the Civil War, share cropping, was not widespread. Less than 10,000 families were still living as share croppers in 1959. This has not meant that life has been easier for colored men and women in Texas, although the larger cities have made efforts to bring about a small degree of integration in recent years. But it has meant a less isolated, less confined life than the brutal closed society of Mississippi. There were fewer people scattered across the countryside of Texas, so they went back and forth more. Since they were scattered so thinly over the dry countryside the rural folk culture didn't develop in the rich depth that it did in the heavy soil of the delta.

The early Texas blues style, like the thin stand of oak to the west of the pine country, was a sparse growth, but it had a rich strain within it, the songs of the slaves that came into the state from the 1850's to the end of the Civil War. It was one of the few areas where the slave songs were still part of the blues, perhaps because there was no strong local growth to crowd out the older verses and styles. In the teeming cabins of the Mississippi delta the older song elements were worked and reworked until the slave music became only a phase in the continuing interaction between the African and the Anglo-American aspects of the musical environment. In Texas, since the population was thinner and more scattered, the songs seemed to retain a more specific nature, almost functioning as a memory of a past that was being handed around from

166

singer to singer, even after the meaning of some of the verses had become lost. In Texas, also, the experience was more recent. When the blues began to take a musical shape there were still men and women who remembered the first years in Texas, and the songs they had sung about it. The most immediate early influence seems to have come from the slave music of northern Alabama, and these song styles have continued to be a presence in the development of the Texas blues.

There was considerable movement within the slave areas during the 1850's, and the drift from Alabama to Texas was a strong one, blowing the Alabama music across the Texas landscape. In the early period of cotton cultivation in Alabama most of the planting was done in the broad valley of the Tennessee River in the north of the state. With increased cultivation, however, prices were driven down - from 30 cents a pound in 1816 to 9 cents a pound in 1829 - and the smaller farmers were forced to sell out and leave. Many of them went south and began clearing land in the more fertile areas in the center of the state, the counties that were to become the "black belt." By the 1850's these men dominated the state's economy. The men who had done the early planting along the Tennessee River had depleted their own soil with continued cotton planting, and poor farming practices had already led to the beginnings of the erosion that was to leave its widening gouge in the red earth. For many of these planters the new state of Texas, which had come into the Union in 1845 as a slave state, was their last hope. They left with their possessions in wagons, their slaves and animals walking along the dusty roads, traveling the hundreds of miles to the open lands of west central Texas. The papers in towns like Huntsville, in northern Alabama, carried hundreds of advertisements like this 1853 notice in the Huntsville *Democrat.*

> "Valuable property for sale - having determined to move to Texas - 1440 acres, 900 cleared..."

As the Civil War turned against the South there was a last effort to get out of the path of the Federal armies, and these forced migrations strengthened the patterns of growth in Texas.

Between 1934 and 1939 the Federal Emergency Relief Administration and the Works Progress Administration made an effort to find and interview the last elderly men and women who had begun their lives as slaves, and among the people who were interviewed there were some who had made the long, difficult trip to Texas. A slave from Georgia remembered,

> "I's born in Georgia, in Norcross, and I's ninety years old. My father's name was Roger Stielszen, and my mother's name was Betty. Massa Earl Stielszen captures them in Africa and brung them to Georgia. He got kilt, and my sister and me went to his son. His son was a killer. He got in trouble there in Georgia and got him two good-stepping horses and the covered wagon. Then he

chains all he slaves round the necks and fastens the chains to the hosses and makes them walk all the way to Texas. My mother and my sister had to walk. Emma was my sister. Somewhere on the road it went to snowing, and Massa wouldn't let us wrap anything round our feet. We had to sleep on the ground, too, in all that snow....

"He come plumb to Austin through that snow. He taken up farming and changes he name to Alex Simpson and changes our names, too. He cut logs and builded he home on the side of them mountains. We never had no quarters. When nighttime come he locks the chain round our necks and then locks it round a tree. Boss, our bed were the ground. All he feed us was raw meat and green corn. Boss, I et many a green weed. I was hungry. He never let us eat at noon, he worked us all day without stopping. We went naked, that the way he worked us. We never had any clothes..."

A slave who was owned by a Baptist minister,

"...The next spring Old Master loaded up again, and we struck out for Texas when the Yankees got too close again. But Master Bill didn't go to Texas, because the Confederates done come that winter and made him go to the army. I think they took him to New Orleans, and Old Master was hopping mad, but he couldn't do anything or they would make him go too, even if he was a preacher...

"...About that time it look like everybody in the world was going to Texas. When we would be going down the road we would have to walk along the side all the time to let the wagons go past, all loaded with folks going to Texas.

"Pretty soon Old Master say, 'Git the wagons loaded again,' and this time we start out with some other people, going north. We go north for awhile and then turn west, and cross the Sabine River and go to Nacogdoches, Texas. Me and my brother Joe and my sister Adeline walked nearly all the way, but my little sister Harriet and my mammy rid in a wagon. Mammy was mighty poorly, and just when we got to the Sabine bottoms she had another baby. Old Master didn't like it 'cause it was a girl, but he named her Texana on account of where she was born and told us children to wait on Mammy good and maybe we would git a little brother next time...

"Old Master's place was right at the corner where Coryell and McLennan and Bosque counties come together, and we raised mostly cotton and just a little corn for feed...

"...if anybody ask me why the Texas Negroes been kept down so much I can tell them. If they set like I did on the bank at that ferry across the Sabine, and see all that long line of covered wagons, miles and miles of them, crossing that river and going west with all they got left out of the war, it ain't hard to understand."

Some of the slaves were brought by ship from the Mississippi plantations through New Orleans and Galveston and the journey became part of the song background of the Texas blues. A slave from Georgia remembered,

> "...Then he...sends us to the port, for to catch the boat. Us gits on that boat and leaves that evening. Coming down the Mississippi 'cross the Gulf, us seed no land for days and days, and us go through the Gulf of Mexico and lands at the port, Galveston, and us comes to Waco on the stagecoach..."

Sixty years later a singer from Dallas named Willard Thomas, "Ramblin'" Thomas, recorded a group of blues for Paramount Records, most of them strongly influenced by commercial recordings. Among his other songs, however, was an older melody using a Mississippi accompaniment style. The guitar was played with a bottleneck or a knife in unison with the voice. The song seems to be a Mississippi field song that was brought into Texas on the boats into Galveston.

Poor boy, poor boy, poor boy long ways from home.

I was down in Louisiana doin' as I please,
Now I'm in Texas I got to work or leave.
Poor boy, poor boy, poor boy long ways from home.

If your home's in Louisiana what you doin' over here?
Said my home ain't in Texas and I sure don't care.
Poor boy, poor boy, poor boy long ways from home.

I don't care if the boat don't never land.
I can stay on the water as long as any man.
Poor boy, poor boy, poor boy long ways from home.

Hey my boat come a rockin' just like a drunken man.
And my home's on the water and I sure don't like land.
Poor boy, poor boy, poor boy long ways from home.

Other slaves were brought by boat up the Red River, and the well known Texas blues, "Red River Blues," may have been first sung during this period. The words are still sung unchanged, though most of the modern singers don't understand their meaning. Country people tell direction by the sun, and someone coming into Texas on the river would orient himself by the change of the sun's direction. From the river's entrance on the Mississippi below Natchez, the boats, with their passengers huddled on the deck, moved first northwest then almost due north. For a slave North was Freedom. Then at Fulton, Arkansas, the river turned due west.

Look where the sun done gone.
Look where the sun done gone.
Look where the sun done gone, poor girl,
Look where the sun done gone.

Yes it's gone God knows where.
Yes it's gone God knows where.
Look where the sun done gone, darling,
Look where the sun done gone.

Now baby, I'm all out and down.
Oh baby, I'm all out and down.
I'm all out and down, I'm (layin' in) this town,
Look where the sun done gone.

I'm a poor boy a long way from home.
Poor boy and a long ways from home.
I'm a poor boy a long way from home, darling,
Look where the sun done gone.

Which way do the Red River run?
Which way do the Red River run?
Which way do the Red River run, poor boy,
Which way do the Red River run?

Yes it runs north and south.
It runs north and south.
Which way do the Red River run, poor boy,
Well it runs north and south.

The swamp land along the Texas coast is rich enough for sugar, and both sides of the Brazos River, west of Houston, are planted with fields of cane. For years the state has maintained prison farms along the Brazos bottoms, and the music in these camps - Ramsey and Retrieve, Central State Farm at Sugarland, Clemens State Farm at Brazoria, Darrington State Farm at Sandy Point - retained many of the characteristics of the African derived slave song that had come into the state in the 1860's. John and Alan Lomax, recording in the camps in the 1930's, found that the prisoners still sang the slow rhythmed choral songs that had almost disappeared everywhere else in the South. The singing was so close to its African derivations that it might even represent an earlier stage of African music than could have been found on the Gold Coast thirty years ago. These camps were less than fifty miles from Houston, and their music was inextricably woven into the texture of the developing blues style. Often similar vocal embellishments were used by both work song leaders and the blues singers, especially slow mordent-like figures based on the equivocal third of the scale. The forms of the work song also made their way into the blues. Often the prison songs alternated a verse by

171

the song leader with a hummed response by the group, and this was often used by Texas country singers, usually as alternate sung and hummed verses. There was even a use of the slow choral song as a blues itself.

The Texas blues of the late 1920's seem to have been influenced by three main streams of music. The first was the body of reels and play party songs of the slavery and post Civil War period, the second the prison work songs, and the third commercial blues recordings. In some of the accompaniment styles there was even a flavor of the white "cowboy" music, and the preference for a high, relatively clear voice might also reflect a white influence. A scattered Negro population was much more susceptible to influence than the more densely populated delta. Before the 1930's the elements of the Texas style were still scattered. Each of the three major areas of Negro song had distinctive melodic and rhythmic characteristics, and many of the best singers could be considered songsters, performers who use a wide range of material without changing its essential elements, instead of the more intensely creative blues singers. The scale patterns also reflected this diversity of influence. The play party songs often used nearly pure diatonic scales, while the prison songs were oriented toward the more African pentatonic and hexatonic groupings. Many of the blues, perhaps because of the influence of commercial recordings, used the conventional city blues scale. It was similar to the delta scales in the ambivalence of the third and the limited use of the second, but there was much more emphasis on the flatted seventh, one of the distinctive characteristics of the city scale patterns.

The rhythms and the accompaniment styles also developed within the framework of the three dominant musical influences. For the "sukey jump" songs the rhythms were in simple binary patterns, the melodic line usually sung without embellishment and the tones clearly defined in pitch. The accompaniments were often "frailed" or "wrapped," that is, in simple chords without finger picking. The rhythms of the work song derived blues, however, were almost completely free. They seemed to be closely related to both the field holler and to the old riverboat "lead line" chants, and the rhythm was an internally stressed chant line. Often the vocal rhythm was almost at complete variance with the accompaniment rhythm; the guitar was silent during the vocal phrase and entered at the end of the sung line. Sometimes the guitar style had a quality of the western white guitar accompaniments and there was considerable stylistic incongruity between the free chant rhythms of the voice and the dance rhythm of the guitar.

The singers using more standard blues material varied considerably in their accompaniments, usually taking elements from the style of the singer from whom they'd learned the song. The knife and bottleneck styles were not widely used, although nearly every singer was able to play at least one knife piece. The style was known, however, and one of

172

the greatest knife players was a Texan, the religious singer Blind Willie Johnson. When the Texas singers began using the flat necked Hawaiian guitar in the 1930's their style seemed to be more influenced by the steel guitar style of the white western orchestras than by the older blues techniques. There was less use of open tunings by the Texas singers and the guitar was usually tuned nearer to concert pitch, rather than the fourth or fifth below it of the Mississippi style.

The Texas guitar style that developed in the 1930's used elements from the older techniques, as well as materials from other blues areas. The form was already roughly shaped by the mid-twenties, and there were recordings using this accompaniment as early as 1926. It was a busy, almost nervous style, more busy than complex. The voice was accompanied with a light, high series of repeated patterns that were distinct from the vocal melody. The harmonic changes were usually regular within the key and the patterns continued through the chord movement. Rhythmically the accompaniment was in three parts, a 4/4 played with the thumb, a brush back by the fingers in a series of 8ths following the thumb note, and - between the vocal phrases - short melodic figures played on the upper strings of the guitar. The steady 4/4 of the bass was rhythmically similar to the Mississippi style. The thumb, however, instead of alternating from the lowest string to a tone a fifth or an octave above it, as in the delta, stayed on the fundamental of the chord, almost invariably on a fretted string at least a fifth above the lowest open string tone. In its earliest recorded forms the accompaniment was still close to the frailed guitar of the country dance songs. As the style developed, however, the voice and the guitar became more closely interrelated. Despite its feeling of nervous busyness the style has emerged as an important accompaniment technique and is widely used by the younger Texas singers.

Pprobably because of the influence of Galveston's sprawling redlight district the piano has also been an important accompaniment instrument in the Texas blues. There was a widespread barrelhouse style related to the ragtime of the years before World War I, and there was also a distinctive blues style that was sometimes known as "fast western." There were strong similarities between the Texas piano and guitar forms, although the keyboard music was essentially pianistic and was more elaborate than the guitar music. There was some use of the walking bass, and the older barrelhouse players used a rudimentary chorded bass similar to the eastern stride pianists, but much of the Texas music used a reiterated open chord in the left hand, usually an open fifth based on the fundamental, alternating with an open sixth. Sometimes the rhythm was doubled, each chord played twice - in eighths - but in slower tempos it had a similarity to the repeated bass note of the guitar accompaniments. The right hand figures were considerably more florid than in the guitar style, and often there was a great deal of rhythmic freedom in the right hand. The voice was usually high, as in the guitar blues, and the accompaniment had the same light, busy quality. During the 'thirties some of the piano patterns were picked up

173

by the guitarists, and in the playing of men like T-Bone Walker there was considerable dexterity on the upper finger board as well as a suggestion of the alternating fifth-sixth chords of the piano bass played on the inner strings of the guitar.

The Texas blues style that emerged from the mingling of its earlier forms of play song, work song, and derivative city blues has some of the thin dryness of the Texas countryside, but it also has a coloring and a shading that is distinctively Texan. The songs themselves are filled with the endless concerns of the blues, eroticism and emotional disappointment, complaint at isolation and poverty, while the singing has some of the high, emotionally veiled mood of the state's western song traditions. The blues meanders across the music of Texas like the rivers across the flat earth of the coastal plain, the water only half covering the gravel of the stream bed, dry and still in the summer heat, but the line of thin trees and cracking mud banks a dusty presence in the Texas landscape.

12. BLIND LEMON JEFFERSON

One of the most difficult of the early Texas singers to place within the Texas musical environment is one of the area's most important blues men and one of the most commercially successful Negro country singers of the 1920's, Blind Lemon Jefferson. Of the more than eighty recordings that he did between 1925 and 1929 only a few use elements of the Texas blues style that emerged in the 1930's. He sometimes used prison songs and chants, but even in these songs his style was more personal than it was characteristic of the area. Perhaps even more significantly, despite his commercial success there was little effort by other singers to imitate him. The young blues men growing up in Dallas and Houston tried to sound like Lonnie Johnson more than they tried to sound like Lemon Jefferson. Sometimes he influenced a particular piece, like Ramblin' Thomas's "No Baby Blues," but there wasn't the pervasive influence on a younger man's style, like Son House's on Robert Johnson. There were similarities in phrasing and in the sound of the voice, but all of the men were from Texas, and they spoke with Texas accents. In his accompaniment styles and his rhythmic concepts, even in some of his themes, Lemon was one of the strongly individual figures of the early blues.

Lemon was born on a small farm outside of Couchman, Texas, a few miles from Wortham in Freestone County. The country is barren and almost flat, with low rolling hills above the grass land. In a description from an earlier sketch of Lemon's life,[1] "...From a small hill near Alec Jefferson's farmhouse at Couchman you can see across the fields to the buildings of Mexia, Texas, twelve miles to the southwest. The scattered buildings of Wortham, Texas, stretch along the railroad tracks five or six miles to the west. There are fields of old oil rigs between the two towns, with gasoline engines still working some of the old wells. The spindly scaffoldings are rusted and weathered. The ground is black with oil waste, but the only signs of oil money in Wortham are three or four ugly church buildings, built out of brick and designed to resemble funeral parlors. Wortham's main street runs three blocks from the Mexia road to the railroad tracks. Most of the buildings are one story brick, with low, overhanging eaves of corrugated iron sheeting. There is one gaudy metal front building from the 1880's, with low relief designs and scrollwork stamped into the thin iron sheets. Wortham is a small market town, a crossroad in lonely country.''

Lemon was born in the summer of 1897, the youngest of the seven children born to Alec Jefferson and his wife, a girl from a neighboring farm named Classie Banks. He began singing when he was a young adolescent. He had been born blind, and there were no other ways he could earn money. Before the First World War, in 1911 or 1912, he was already coming into Wortham to sing, and by the time he was twenty he was singing for parties and country dances throughout the county. He went into Dallas about 1917, and lived there for nearly ten years, though he spent months out singing in the cotton country south of the city. His cousin, Alec Jefferson, rememberd him coming to Waxahatchie to sing for "country suppers."

> *Of course, my mother didn't let me go to them country suppers often. They was rough. Men was hustling women and selling bootleg and Lemon was singing for them all night. They didn't even do any proper kind of dancing, just stompin'.*
>
> *They'd go down to the station and get him in the afternoon. He'd start singing about eight and go on until four in the morning. Sometime he'd have another fellow with him, playing a mandolin or a guitar and singing along, but mostly it would be just him, sitting there playing and singing all night.*[2]

One of the singers who worked with him a few times was the folk singer Huddie Ledbetter, who was in prison most of the time that Lemon was in Dallas, but remembered singing with him in the Dallas brothels. Lemon was widely known for his music, and he finally did well enough to get a car and a driver. He married a girl named Roberta in 1922 or 1923 and a son was born two or three years later. He sometimes went back to the farm with his wife, letting his driver give rides to the girls in town. He seemed to have traveled as far east as Mississippi and Alabama, and many older blues men remember hearing him when they were in towns like Jackson and Memphis. In 1925, when the rush to girl blues singers had begun to slow down, the companies turned to the men singers, and it was only a few months before Paramount found Lemon Jefferson.

Dallas was already a growing and active city in the mid-twenties, and there was sporadic recording activity there for several years, mostly through the efforts of a local music store owner who, like Jesse Johnson in St. Louis and H. C. Spears in Jackson, worked as a talent scout for the Chicago and New York companies. He did a test recording of Lemon's singing with a portable machine that had been set up in the rug department of a local furniture store sometime in the spring of 1925, and sent it up to Mayo Williams at Paramount. Mayo brought him up to Chicago sometime late in 1925 or early in 1926 for the first of the many sessions Lemon was to do for the company in the next three and a half years.

"Here's a real old-fashioned blues by a real old-fashioned blues singer - Blind Lemon Jefferson from Dallas. This 'Booster Blues' and 'Dry Southern Blues' on the reverse side are two of Blind Lemon's old-time tunes. With his singing he plays the guitar in real southern style."

The ad ran in the *Chicago Defender* on April 3, 1926. There had been a few earlier recordings by country blues men, Ed Andrews, Daddy Stovepipe, Papa Charlie Jackson, but Lemon was considerably more successful than they had been. Two or three of his recordings were among the most widely sold country blues releases of the 1920's, even though the style of the first recordings was so raw and uncompromising that it is difficult to think of them as commercial releases by a commercial company. It was as rough and as individual as any of the music that field collectors were to find in the South in the next forty years of recording. His style was, in some ways, so distinctive because it was a hybrid of the influences on him. Some of the style, the vocal phrasing and the few regular rhythms, was in part from the Alabama styles still sung in Freestone County, but some of the melodies and characteristic patterns were from the commercial recordings by the women blues singers of the early 1920's. His harmonic structure was the usual I-IV-V of the city blues, he generally used the conventional three line verse form, and often his texts were concerned with the usual "leaving trains" and "mistreating women" of the commercial blues song.

But if his blues sometimes were tangled with the conventional melodies and texts his singing style and his accompaniment rhythms were considerably different from the city recordings. The high, clear sound of his voice, despite the inadequate acoustical recording techniques, had a startling intensity, and he kept the freely structured rhythms of the field holler and the Texas gang chant in his guitar. The accompaniments, especially on "Dry Southern Blues," were very complex, and the relationship between the guitar and the voice was very loose. Often he sounded as though he were singing to himself while somebody else played a few tentative phrases on the guitar. His vocal line was very irregular and the guitar only occasionally tried to hold it within the 4/4 rhythm of the usual blues measure. The guitar style had some of the elements of country white "frailing," but because of the tension of the vocal line the patterns were often wildly unpredictable. He was one of the few country musicians who seemed to rely on improvisation in his accompaniments. It was a desolate, lost sound, the voice tinged with loneliness, the restless guitar moving below it as though it were looking for a phrase or a run to end its incessant movement. Although the change from acoustical to electrical recording in 1927 gave his voice more presence, there was little change in his style in the Paramount recordings. His voice darkened, and his accompaniments became less hurried, but his last session, in the fall of 1929, was as direct and as compelling as his first had been more than three years before.

In his recordings he drew on a number of sources for his songs. There were even enough folk and gospel performances to suggest that, like Charley Patton, he was almost as much of a songster as he was a blues singer. He sang for every kind of social function in the Texas back country, and he must have had a wide repertoire of hymns and play songs, as well as his blues. When the younger Texas singer, Lightning Hopkins, first heard Lemon he was singing for a Baptist picnic at Buffalo, Texas, and he would not have sung "Oil Well Blues" or "Black Snake Moan" for a church gathering. Lightning's description catches some of the feeling of what it must have been like to hear Lemon out in the country where he had been born and raised.

> *... I went to the Buffalo Association with my guitar and I run up on Blind Lemon Jefferson. He had a crowd of people around him and I was standing there looking at him play and I just went to playing my guitar just what he was playing. So he say, "Who's that playing that guitar?" So they say, "Oh, that's just a little boy here knocking on the guitar." He says, "No, he's playing that guitar," says, "Where he at? Come here, boy." And I went on over there where he was and he's feeling for me and I was so low he reached down and says, "This here is what was picking that guitar?" They say, "Yeah." So he said, "Do that again." So I did, the little note again, the same one he done. He said, "Well, that's my note," says, "that's the same thing. Boy, you keep that up you gonna be a good guitar player." So he went on and he commenced to playing; so I went to playing right on with him. So I was so little and low the peoples couldn't see me and we was standing by a truck. They put me up on top of the truck, and Blind Lemon was standing down by the truck. And me and him, man, we carried it on...* [3]

Lemon was restricted by his market, since he began recording when the commercial interest was in the conventional city blues, but he was still able to sing Texas folk songs and minstrel show pieces, as well as country hymns and gospel songs. It seems probable that the Paramount gospel releases by "Deacon L. J. Bates" were recordings that Lemon had done, and Paramount used a pseudonym for him as they had for Patton. Two of the songs are very similar to Lemon's usual style, "He Arose From The Dead" and "Where Shall I Be?", although there is almost a self-consciousness in the rhythm and the voice. He recorded one of the earliest versions of the folk gambling song "Jack O' Diamonds," and many Texas blues men remember his version of the well known "Two White Horses In A Line." It was renamed "See That My Grave Is Kept Clean" for the recording, a 1927 release on Paramount 12585, but it was the same folk melody and most of the verses that were sung not only in Texas but in many other areas of the South. The melody was used by most of the Mississippi singers and was found east of the Appalachians in the Carolinas and Georgia.

Probably because he had learned it as a folk melody Lemon's performance of it was much less irregular than most of his blues, but he wasn't consistent in his use of folk song materials. His third release included "Corinna Blues," his reworking of the song "See See Rider," and it was as free as his most irregular blues pieces. The "Black Horse Blues" on the other side of the record, Paramount 12367, included a variation on the verse that was usually associated in Mississippi with Charley Patton.

> Well, get my black horse and saddle up my black mare,
> Well, get my black horse and saddle up my black mare.
> I'm going over to my good girl, she's in the world somewhere.

Following the success of his "Black Snake Moan" in the winter of 1926 he spent a few weeks working as an OKeh record artist, and did a session for them on March 14, 1927. The only release from the session was a new version of "Black Snake Moan" and "Match Box Blues" on OKeh 8455, but he also did other folk material, and one of the songs was a version of the "Elder Green - Alabama Bound - Don't You Leave Me Here" melody, with the title "Elder Green's In Town." It was close to Patton's version of the piece in both melody and verses, and the similarity strengthens the impression that there were close ties between his music and the field blues of the Alabama and north Mississippi area.

Example 25

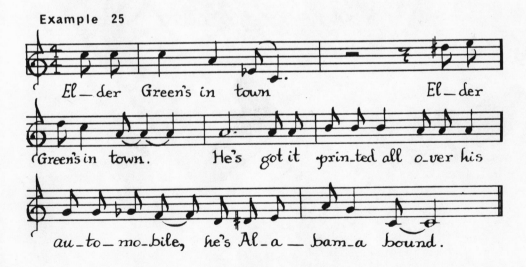

The first verse was the most interesting, with its bridge from the Elder Green song, which has the feeling of an older minstrel tune, to the Alabama Bound phrase. He returned to Elder Green in the last verse, ending with rough country irreverence.

179

Elder Green's in town, Elder Green's in town,
    Elder Green's in town,
He's got it printed all over his automobile he's Alabama bound.

Don't worry me, don't worry me again.
When I get drunk and all down and out don't worry me.

I've got a high brown and she's long and tall.
Lord, lord, lord, lord, boys, she'll make a panther squall.

Elder Green don't care, Elder Green don't care.
He's gonna tear down the old Church of God and build a
    barrelhouse there.

He also did his only recorded instrumental at the session, a ragtime
guitar piece with the title "English Stop Time." Like "Elder Green's
In Town," it was closely related to music from the older slave areas
of the south east.

Example 26

Unlike Patton, however, he did not use much of the local countryside in his blues. In the town of Wortham three or four people still laughed over his piece that mentioned the nearby town of Groesbeck. A man standing in a small store warmed his hands over the coal stove thinking about Lemon's songs. "There was one he did about Groesbeck, about going to the penitentiary. I never did forget that one." The song "Blind Lemon's Penitentiary Blues," was one of the few in which Lemon referred to the towns near the farm where he had grown up.

> Take Fort Worth for your dressing and Dallas (?) for your style.
> Take Fort Worth for your dressing and Dallas (?) for your style.
> But if you want to go to the state penitentiary go to
>   Groesbeck for your trial.

> I hung around Groesbeck, I worked in hard showers of rain.
> I say I hung around Groesbeck, worked in hard showers
>   of rain.
> I never felt the least bit uneasy 'til I caught that penitentiary
>   train.

> I used to be a drunkard, rowdy everywhere I go.
> I say I used to be a drunkard and rowdy everywhere I go.
> If ever I get out of this trouble I'm in I won't be rowdy no more...

Lemon does not seem to have been in prison himself, but like every great singer his blues were a reflection of the emotional concerns of the people who were his audience. He was able, as the St. Louis singer Henry Townsend expressed it, to take "...sympathy with the fellow..." He sang a "Lock Step Blues," a "Hangman's Blues," a "'Lectric Chair Blues," and the brilliant "Prison Cell Blues," which kept the two line poetic form and the shouted melodic outline of the prison gang song.

Example 27

Many of his images were also taken from his country background, even though he had grown up without sight. Throughout his recording career he remained a Texas singer, despite the years he spent in Chicago and his trips to Memphis and Jackson.

He sang every kind of song, and his blues were an expression of nearly every aspect of the life that went on in the cabins along the winding stream beds and the oil blackened dirt roads, but there was also a personal emphasis in his music. He was as tormented with sexuality as the young Robert Johnson. His women, his "rider," his "brown," or his "pigmeat," dominated his blues. Desire with Lemon was hurried and impatient.

> ...I'm crazy about my light bread and my pigmeat on the side.
> I say I'm crazy about my light bread and my pig meat on the side.
> But if I taste your jelly roll I be satisfied.

> I want to know if your jelly roll's fresh, if your jelly roll's
>   stale.
> Well, I want to know if your jelly roll's fresh, if your jelly
>   roll's stale.
> I'm going to haul off and buy me some if I have to break it loose
>   in jail...

> (Bakershop Blues)

> I feel like jumping through the keyhole in your door.
> I feel like jumping through the keyhole in your door.
> If you jump this time, baby, you won't jump no more.

> (Mean Jumper Blues)

His sexual blues were often intense performances, and their physical yearning was expressed with a repetitive insistence. His most successful recording was a vivid sexual blues. In May, 1926, a young girl singer from north of Dallas, Victoria Spivey, recorded a piece that she called "Black Snake Blues" for Okeh Records in St. Louis. Miss Spivey insists that the song had no sexual overtones, and that it described something that had happened to a girl friend when a black snake, a common field snake in Texas, crawled into the cabin where the girl was living. When Lemon recorded it six months later as "That Black Snake Moan" she remembers, with some resentment, that "...he changed it into a sex song." He included the image of the black snake crawling into his room, but he changed the verse, and with the change the song became a crying sexual lament

> Um - um, black snake crawling in my room.
> Um - um, black snake crawling in my room.
> Yes, some pretty mama better get this black snake soon.

> Uum - what's the matter now?
> Uum - what's the matter now?
> Yes, some pretty mama better get this black snake soon.
>
> Well, I wonder where this black snake's gone.
> I wonder where this black snake's gone.
> Lord, that black snake, mama, done run my mama home..

His obvious reference to the penis was more openly sexual than was usual in the early blues, and the record was also one of his best performances. He used a direct, assertive melodic line and his voice was even more intense than on many of the recordings he had done earlier in the year. It was the success of his first "Blacksnake" that led to OKeh's efforts to get him away from Paramount and the recordings of "Elder Green's In Town" and "English Stop Time." He was recording for Paramount again within a few weeks of the OKeh sessions and in June, 1927, he did a second "Blacksnake" piece, "Black Snake Dream Blues." In 1929 there was still another piece using the same imagery, "That Black Snake Moan No. 2." In these later pieces he consciously used the sexual symbolism of the snake, unlike the first recording which has some of the feeling of a spontaneous improvisation while he was recording. Paramount, however, never intimated in their advertising that Lemon was talking about anything but a snake. There were even drawings of Lemon and the snakes to make the point more strongly. To the people who bought the records, though, the symbolism was obvious.

> ...Uum, better find my mama soon.
> Uum, better find my mama soon.
> I woke up this morning black snake was makin' (just a) ruckus
>   in my room.
>
> Black snake is evil, black snake is all I see.
> Black snake is evil, black snake is all I see.
> I woke up this morning he was moved in on me.
>
> Uum, black snake was hanging 'round.
> Uum, black snake was hanging 'round.
> He occupied my living room and broke my (folding bed?) down.
>
>   (That Black Snake Moan No. 2)

During his years of recording Lemon also seems to have traveled extensively, although his movements were vague and difficult to trace. He still went back to the farm at Couchman for visits, although his family saw little of him after he began working in Chicago. He had become one of Paramount's most established singers, despite the uncompromising roughness of his style. In the spring of 1928 the company even issued a birthday record for him, with a beautiful gray and yellow label that had his picture and a streamer saying "Happy Birthday,

Lemon." The necessity to find new material sometimes left him with thinly derivative verses, or with blues that were confused and incomplete. In a piece like "Balky Mule Blues" he began with verses about a balky mule and then included verses from a "Bear Cat Blues" before he was finished. Also he was sometimes used to "cover" successful recordings by other artists. Like most singers who were recording extensively during this period he did a flood blues, "Rising High Water Blues," to cover Bessie Smith's "Back Water Blues." It was one of three blues that he did with the pianist George Perkins as accompanist. He also did a "Chinch Bug Blues" to cover Lonnie Johnson's "Mean Old Bed Bug", and a "How Long How Long" after Leroy Carr's recording. In all of his recordings, however, despite the thinness of some of the verses, the musical level was consistently high.

Some singers drift like clouds over the flat landscape, changing with every movement of the wind. Lemon changed very little during the years when he was recording. He used the three line verse form for most of the blues and there was a consistency to his melodic and rhythmic approach. He left the folk songs and the hymns in their original form, and there were occasional pieces like "Bad Luck Blues" that are difficult to fit into any category, but the rest were strongly stamped with his individual style. "Bad Luck Blues" had some of the style of a play party song or a medicine show piece.

Sugar you catch that Katy, I'll catch that Santa Fe,
    Doggone my bad luck soul,
Sugar you catch that Katy and I'll catch that Santa Fe.
I mean Santy, speaking of Fe,
    When you get in Dallas, pretty mama, look around for me.

He used only a handful of melodies for his blues pieces, one of the most distinctive melodies one with a final phrase in the accompaniment moving to a harmony on the VI of the scale. Blues with this melody included some of his best performances, among them "Tin Cup Blues," "Mean Jumper Blues," and "Sunshine Special." He also used a melodic phrase that descended from V to IV in the last line for blues like "Oil Well Blues" and "Pneumonia Blues." His more or less conventional three line verse forms differed most importantly in the phrasing of the second line. In some blues - "Big Night Blues" and "Peach Orchard Mama" - the last word of the second line was delayed as a kind of halting resolution, in others the phrasing was more regular.

Although Lemon largely remained outside of the main areas of development of the Texas blues he sometimes used many of the elements which were to become part of the mature style. In "Stocking Feet Blues" he used the rythmically insistent guitar bass and the elaborate upper string patterns that were also characteristic of some of the pieces of Henry Thomas, and he developed a rudimentary compound verse, a verse form that was to become almost a characteristic of the later blues of men like Lightning Hopkins. The harmonic resolution was still unsettled, but the verse itself was almost the fully developed compound stanza.

> She got up this morning,
> Come a tippin' 'cross the floor,
> Said mama,
> In her stocking feet,
> Honey, fare thee, sweet papa, fare thee well.
> I done all in the world I could, trying to get along with you.

"Tippin'" is a country term for "tiptoeing."

The scale in Lemon's blues was usually an open pentatonic, but in some of his strongest pieces the scale used only the first, an altered third, a fifth, an altered seventh and the octave. For the more song-like pieces, even a prison song like "Prison Cell Blues," the scale was fuller, omitting only the second.

Lemon seems to have done his last recordings for Paramount at the Gennett Studios in Richmond, Indiana, on September 24, 1929. He did eight blues, all of them among his finest performances. The Gennett Studio had a much better sound than the thin and poorly balanced sound of the Paramount Studio in Port Washington; so there was also much more immediacy and presence on the releases than on some of his earlier recordings. There was Lemon's usual sexual preoccupation in "Bakershop Blues," with its elaborately developed jellyroll image, and a bitter infidelity blues, "Pneumonia Blues." Perhaps one of the most moving of all Lemon's songs was the fourth blues of the session, "That Crawling Baby Blues," which expressed a disturbed, muted anguish over the confused personal relationships around him. He began, as usual, with the specific moment,

> Well, the baby crying, up to his mama's knee.
> Well, the baby crying, up to his mama's knee.
> Cryin' about his sweet milk and she won't feed him just his cream.

but the moment was left unfinished, not as a narrative, but as an emotional reality which could justify the generalized verse which usually followed the opening verse in Lemon's blues. There was also some ambivalence in his use of terms that could be mistaken for sexual imagery, "sweet milk," "she won't feed him just his cream." He extended his description in the second verse, however, definitely setting the blues into an infidelity context.

> Well, he cryin' in the fireplace and stops in the middle of the floor.
> Well, he cryin' from the fireplace and stops in the middle of the
> floor.
> Say mama, ain't that your second daddy standin' back there in the
> (?) door.

And with the third verse he finally set the emotional moment in one of the few blues verses that considered the effect of infidelity on the children growing up in the emotional confusion of casual promiscuity.

> Well, she grabbed my baby and spanked him, I tried to make her
>   leave him alone.
> Well, she grabbed my baby and spanked him, I tried to make her
>   leave him alone.
> I tried my best to stop her and she said the baby ain't none of mine.

The fourth verse, the generalized statement, was built from the emotional situation of the other verses.

> The woman rocks the cradle and I declare she rules the home.
> Woman rocks the cradle and I declare she rules the home.
> Many man rocks some other man's baby and the fool thinks
>   he's rocking his own.

The final verse was obviously padding to round out the performance.

> Well, it was late last night when I learnt the crawling baby blues.
> I said it was late last night when I learnt the crawling baby blues.
> My woman threw my clothes out doors and now I got the crawling
>   baby blues.

There were few blues which so completely controlled the emotional elements in the blues form, and it was as effective melodically as it was textually.

Example 28

Lemon was also to be part of a Paramount release using several of the company's most popular blues artists - a "hometown skiffle" record advertised in the *Defender* on February 22, 1930 - but he died some-time before the recording session. There is still considerable confusion over his death, and it will probably always be difficult to reconstruct the events that led to it. Son House has said that he met Lemon in the studio in Port Washington the day before Son recorded in July, 1930, and that the next morning, when he, Patton, and Louise Johnson came to the studio to begin recording, they were met by the recording director, Art Satterlee, who shook his head and said, "I've got some bad news for you. Lemon was killed in a car accident early this morning." Four months before this, however, Walter Taylor and John Byrd recorded "Wasn't It Sad About Lemon?", and Reverend Emmett Dickinson did a "Death of Blind Lemon," both released on Paramount 12945 in the early spring, so Lemon must have been dead for several months before Son went to Chicago. A Paramount employee named Aleatha Robinson remembered that Lemon was recording on the afternoon before his death, but he may only have been in the Paramount offices on business. "Wasn't It Sad About Lemon?" suggested that the story the family was told of his death was probably true.

> Blind Lemon was born in Texas,
> A state we all know well.
> 'Twas on the streets of Chicago,
> Was where poor Lemon fell....
>
> The weather was below zero
> On the day he passed away,
> But this is the truth we all know well.
> That's a debt we all have to pay...

The family and friends in Texas heard that he froze to death in Chicago, and John Steiner, the Chicago jazz historian and business man who bought the Paramount property in the 1940's, heard from people associated with the company that Lemon had left the studios late in the afternoon, gone to play for a party, and been found dead on the street early in the morning with the snow drifted over his body. No one was able to tell him what happened to Lemon during the night although there was a suggestion that Lemon might have had a heart attack as he was waiting for his car and driver to pick him up. There was also a story that Lemon left the party drunk and got lost as he tried to make his way through the streets in the cold winter night. The wind sweeps in on Chicago from the lake, and on bitter winter nights it will almost turn a man around as he walks, stinging his face with fine driven crystals of ice and numbing his body through the heaviest clothes. Paramount hired a Texas pianist who was working for them, Will Ezell, to go with the body back to Dallas, and the funeral was held in Wortham with Lemon's family and neighbors walking across the cold, frozen fields to get to the services. He was buried in a country cemetery outside of Wortham, and, like Patton's, his grave was not marked. The neighbors remembered, however, that his mother had been buried next to Lemon when she died in 1947. Her headstone, a simple concrete monument, is under a small tree just inside a rusting barbed wire fence in the lonely cemetery, only a rusting metal marker in the wild grass growing over the space beside her grave.

13. HENRY THOMAS, "RAGTIME TEXAS"

The songster tradition was as deeply rooted in the spindly valleys of east central Texas as the work songs and the blues of Lemon Jefferson. Most singers in the South were called "songsters" by their neighbors because they usually could be prevailed upon to make music at almost any occasion, from a church picnic to a children's party. Nearly every blues singer did this kind of entertaining in his own community and had a few church songs and party songs in his repertoire. The difference between these songs and his blues was that he usually sang these pieces more or less as he had learned them, unlike his personal blues. It was the easy familiarity of the other pieces that made them effective for little dances and parties. The singers, also, were often brought to white affairs, when they would be surrounded by an audience that had to have old songs and considerable servility. In nearly every southern community there is an older performer who can be hired for white parties and social occasions like debuts and horse shows. Usually he is also his own community's "songster," and he knows dozens of songs like "It Ain't Gonna Rain No More," "My Blue Heaven," and "The Wreck of the Old 97." Because of the influence of local speech patterns and guitar techniques the style often has many of the characteristics of the blues style of the area, even though the songs are known everywhere in the South. In Texas the songsters had the high, tense sound of the blues singers, and their songs, like the weeds along the winding, dry stream beds near Austin or San Antonio, had the smell of the Texas dust and wind.

One of the most extensively recorded of the early Texas male singers was a songster named Henry Thomas, also called "Ragtime Texas" on some of the records. He was skilled performer, often reminiscent of one of the best known of the Memphis medicine show singers, Jim Jackson. Nothing is known of Thomas' life, and, as is often true with songsters, nothing can be learned from his songs. The blues singer has to expose himself as a person in his blues, but the songster is more

190

a reflection of an area's musical interests than he is of his own concerns. Thomas mentions the town of Huntsville in the song "Run Molly Run," using the verse,

> I went down to Huntsville, I did not go to stay,
> I just got there in good old time to wear that ball and chain.

Huntsville is on Route 75 north of Houston, and there is a state penitentiary there, but the verse is a conventional one in the area. It could even refer to the Huntsville in northern Alabama. Thomas was one of the first artists used by the recording director Mayo Williams after he left Paramount Records and moved to Vocalion in 1927. The sessions were done in Chicago between July, 1927, and October, 1929. The releases were well advertised, but the copy material had no personal information. In the picture used for the ads he looked in his late thirties or early forties, his hair graying, his expression guardedly professional.

Thomas was an interesting singer for the range of his songs as well as his accompaniment styles, and he was also interesting for his use of the instrument known as the "quills." He was probably the first singer to record using the quills, even though they were at one time widely played throughout the South. The instrument is also known by the technical term "syrinx," but it probably is most widely known as "panpipes." Each "pipe" is a cross blown cane reed, held against the lips while the player blows across the opening in the top, just as a child blows on an empty bottle. The pitch of the reed is determined by its length - the shorter the reed the higher the sound - and usually the player binds a group of them together in a row, holding them together with pieces of stick. They are usually tuned to the local folk scale, and Thomas tuned his to a e-#f-a-b-c#e' scale, even though most of the songs he did were in a more generally diatonic mode. In the picture that was used in the advertisements the quills seem to be enclosed in a dark colored box that hangs around his neck on a rack similar to the arrangement that harmonica players use. Some of the finest of his recordings were characterized by the light piping sound of the quills alternating verses with his voice.

Thomas seems to have been almost a pure songster. Once he'd learned a song he didn't change it, even if he'd only half learned it at the beginning. In a song that seems to be derived from an earlier recording by one of the city women singers, "Woodhouse Blues," he even left the terms of endearment unchanged, and sang "Daddy, daddy .." instead of changing it to something which would make more sense. In some of the songs that he learned from white sources he had difficulties with the harmonies as well. In "The Little Red Caboose," which sounds like a minstrel tune, and "Honey, Won't You Allow Me One More Chance," which sounds like a vaudeville piece, he missed obvious chord changes, and in one of the country pieces, "When The Train Comes Along," he sounded in places as though he were singing in one key and accompanying himself in another. He does not seem to have had a strong musical sense. A songster,

191

however, is important for what he remembers, rather than what he creates, and some of the songs Thomas remembered had the loose, noisy exuberance of the country picnics or the church suppers where he must have heard them.

Nearly every folk blues from the Texas - Louisiana area found its way into the songs he recorded. One of his pieces, "Bob McKinney," is a medley of folk blues, beginning with a version of "Stackolee," using Bob McKinney as the hero; then it goes into "Take Me Back," "Make Me A Pallet On Your Floor," and "Bully Of The Town." However, he didn't record "Jack O'Diamonds," even though it was widely known in Texas. He tended to turn away from the darker glints of Texas music, as though he were concerned more with a country white audience than with a blues audience. He must have played for dancing, and in his "Old Country Stomp" there were even verses with dance calls.

> Get your partners, promenade, promenade all around now...
> Oh boy you started wrong, take your partners, promenade...

One piece he remembered, "Shanty Blues," might have been from one of the states to the east, and it had a heavier sound than some of his other pieces. For the accompaniment he used an open tuning and played with a knife or a bottleneck. Most of the verses were conventional, but there were other verses which must have been from part of an older work song. The melody was a four line strain like the country dance pieces, but the work song fragments stuck to it like a burr caught in a man's overalls as he moves through the dry autumn brush along the banks of the Trinity River.

> Dogs on my track, man on his horse,
> Make it to my shanty if I can,
> If I can, if I can,
> Make it to my shanty if I can.

His voice was the high, less intense Texas voice, the tone produced further forward in the mouth than the Mississippi singers, the melodic line with little embellishment. His tone was a little heavier than some of the other Texas singers, perhaps because he was a little older when he began to record. Many of his pieces were the kind of song that Huddie Ledbetter, a Louisiana singer who spent years playing in Texas, called "sukey jump" pieces, little repetitive melodies that had an almost childish simplicity and innocence.

Example 29

192

run Mol—ly   run —   let us have some fun.

Cher—ry,   Cher—ry,   cher—ry like a   rose—.

I love that pret—ty yel—low gal,   God al—migh—ty   Knows.

In the best of his blues there was this same musical brightness, even though the texts were often sombre.

Example 30

(Texas Easy Street Blues)
♩ = 180

Um — m —   what's the mat—ter   now.—

te—ll — me   ma—ma   what's the mat—ter

now. —   I'm   goin' back   to Tex—as,

live   on   ea—sy   street.

His accompaniments were generally as simple as the songs. For pieces like "The Fox And The Hounds" he used a "frailing" accompaniment, letting the excitement come from his yipping voice, the little melody of the pipes, and the verses of the song. On the pieces in which he used the quills the accompaniments were even less complex. He usually limited himself to "wrapping the guitar" - playing in straight beats - and the sound was often discordant, as though he were using unconventional finger positions. Like most Texas singers he kept the guitar close to standard pitch, instead of slackened considerably below it, as in

193

HENRY THOMAS ADVERTISEMENTS

Mississippi. Also he played in the middle strings to a great extent. There were other techniques that he also shared with later Texas singers, and he could be considered one of the earliest Texas blues men as well as a songster. Three of his recorded pieces, "Texas Worried Blues," "Cotton Field Blues," and "Texas Easy Street Blues," had nearly all the elements that became part of the emerging Texas blues style. The voice was unforced, and the melody, although close to the conventional city blues melody, was faster and lighter. The accompaniment technique was one of the first to completely define the Texas guitar style. There were elemer's of it in some of the Lemon Jefferson recordings, but in the Thoma pieces the style was more fully realized. The thumb played a repetitive 4/4 on the tonic of the key, the sound light and insistent. Usually there was the brush back on the upper strings with the first fingers, and a melodic figure was picked against this background up the neck of the guitar. Thomas might have been the first to play in this style, although it seems unlikely that he could have created it. It was probably a blues that the songster remembered, just as he remembered his other pieces.

Little of what Thomas sang continued in the Texas blues traditions, and he is a half-forgotten figure in the development of Texas music. Through Thomas, however, it is clear that the music of Texas has its own line of development going back almost as far as the earliest Mississippi style, going back, at least, to the point when the songster Henry Thomas first heard and remembered it.

TEXAS ALEXANDER

14. "TEXAS" ALEXANDER

Lightning Hopkins first met his cousin Alger Alexander in the early 1930's at a baseball game in a small town not far from Lightning's town of Centerville.

Well, I met Texas Alexander in Leon County at a place you call Normangee, Texas. They had a little old do down there, what you call, I don't know, a picnic, and they had a ball game, see. Well, Normangee was playing Leona, so that's the way they had them named, they didn't, you know, no special big names like they got now ... just Leona playing Normangee. So I got down there and ... I seen a man standing up on a truck with his hand up to his mouth and, man, that man was singing. That was Texas, my cousin, I didn't know. Alright, I goes on there and that man was singing so and he like to broke up the ball game. People was paying so much attention to him instead of the ball game. Well, he had been gone. All his people was living in Normangee, most of them, you know, his mother and them at that time was living, and he had been gone kind of like I did and stayed for a while and he come back. That's the way he come back, you understand, he come back ready. I mean he come back ready with that singing. He couldn't play no music. He never played an instrument in his life. But he'd tote a guitar. He'd buy a guitar, and he'd tote it in case that he'd run up on you or me or somebody could play and he'd sing. And he kept a guitar 'cause if he asked could you play a guitar and you said, "Yeah," well, he got one, see. And then you all come tear it off. And that's when I met Texas Alexander many years ago in Normangee, Texas.

I accompanied him for quite a bit there in Crockett, Texas, Grapeland, Patterstein, Oakwood, and Buffalo and Centerville, Normangee, Flynn, and Marquez and back in them places. I never followed Texas no further than Houston for a long way, 'cause he was a man to get up and go. First Cadillac that I ever known to be, you know, one of them expensive, bad cars - he went somewhere and he come to Normangee in a Cadillac and it was the longest old ugly car, old long Cadillac, one of them there old first made. But it was new! He got over there and everybody admired him, you know, because colored people didn't have nothing. They didn't even have T-Model Fords then and you know he come in a Cadillac. Yeah, Texas was doing all right for himself... [1]

Texas Alexander's music, like Blind Lemon Jefferson's and Henry Thomas's, was distinctly a part of the Texas landscape, but his singing was an individual expression. Many of his pieces were strongly influenced by the conventional city blues recordings, but in his most characteristic blues there was a rich imagery and a melodic expressiveness derived from one of the root sources of Texas music, the work songs and prison chants. Like Lemon he was commercially directed by the blues market, and he did few of the country play songs or ballads of a songster like Henry Thomas, but unlike Lemon he had developed his vocal style without accompaniment, so the work songs had undergone fewer rhythmic changes in their adaptation to the blues. He was in prison in the '30's, but it is not known if he was a convict before he began recording. Some of the work songs that he used were sung in the hilly countryside around Normangee and he could have learned them as a young man working in the fields. Others may have been derived from the ''lead line'' songs sung by the caller working the steamships as he dropped his weighted line from the ship's bow to find out how much water was under the shallow hull. There was a use of words and phrases from the river songs which could have come from the men working the landing stages on the rivers, or from the work gangs that were building levees for flood control.

It was the long, almost chanted melodic line of the holler which left the deepest imprint on his style, rather than the stronger gang shouts. The rhythm was a sensed pulse that was very difficult for an accompanist to follow, even though there was a consistent accent pattern in each of the verses.

Example 31

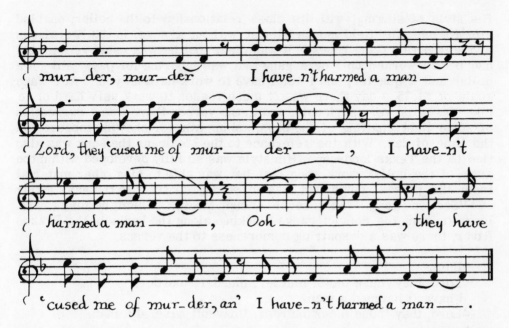

mur_der, mur_der   I have_n't harmed a man___

Lord, they 'cused me of mur___ der___,   I have_n't

harmed a man___,   Ooh___,   they have

'cused me of mur-der, an' I have_n't harmed a man___.

The verses themselves were often taken directly from specific field songs, and his soft, often hummed vocal tone had some of the feeling of a man singing as he bent over a cotton chopping hoe.

I been working on the section, section 32.
I'll get a dollar and a quarter, and I won't have to work hard as you.
Lord, I'll get a dollar and a quarter and I won't have to
    work hard as you.

Oh nigger licks 'lasses and the white man likes it too.
Lord, I wonder what in the world is the Mexican going to do.
Oh the nigger licks 'lasses and the white man likes it too.

Oh captain, captain, what's the matter with you.
If you got any battleaxe please, sir, give me a chew.
Oh captain, captain, what's the matter with you.

Water boy, water boy, bring your water 'round.
'Til you ain't got no water, fetch your bucket down.
Water boy, water boy, bring your water 'round.

Oh captain, captain, what time of day.
Oh he looked at me and he walked away.
Uum, oh captain, what's the matter with you?

If you got any battleaxe, battleaxe, please, sire, give me a chew.
Uum.
Uum, lord, oh lord, oh lord.

(Section Gang Blues)

199

His style of singing, with its close relationship to the holler, enabled him to use the field songs almost without change. In the literalness of the "Section Gang Blues," it was clear that he was using verses that had been "worked up" by a gang that was laboring for pay, "I'll get a dollar and a quarter, and I won't have to work hard as you." At a wage scale of $1.25 a day there wasn't much reason to work very hard or to take the work very seriously, and in the verses there was a suggestion of some light chaffing of the boss, asking him for chewing tobacco and the time of day. With the reference to the Mexicans the song was also tied to the Texas landscape. His style was so fully developed within the area of the holler work song that he was able to sing other material from the prison gangs that was in strong contrast to the easy joking of "Section Gang." In "Levee Camp Moan," which he might have learned from the convict gangs working along the banks of the Brazos River, there was a despairing sombreness to the verses.

Uum,
Lord, they 'cuse me of murder, murder, murder.
I haven't harmed a man.
Lord, they 'cuse me of murder, I haven't harmed a man.

Uum,
They 'cused me of forgery and I can't write my name.
Lord, they have 'cused me of forgery and I can't write my name.

I went all around the whole corral,
I couldn't find a mule with its shoulder (bare?)
Lord,

Uum,
I worked all mornin' and I worked
And I couldn't find a mule with its shoulder (bare.)

Oh, she went up the country but she's on my mind.
Oh, she went up the country but she's on my mind.

Oh, if you don't come on the big boat she better not land.
Lord, if you don't come on the big boat, big boat,
I mean she better not land.

Nearly all of these verses had been used by a number of blues singers, but there were few recordings in which they were still so closely related to their work song form. These two blues, on OKeh 8498, were the first songs of Alexander's to be released, but through the rest of his career there were only a handful of releases with their distinctiveness. For nearly all of his early sessions the accompanist was the guitar player and blues singer Lonnie Johnson, who developed a free guitar style to accompany the slow field chants, and their first duets were richly musical. Before his early recording career ended Alexander had been accompanied by Lonnie, by Lonnie and the white jazz guitarist

200

Eddie Lang, the Mississippi Sheiks, a Texas guitarist named Little Hat Jones, the pianist Eddie Heywood, and a trio composed of the great New Orleans cornetist King Oliver, Eddie Lang, and the pianist Clarence Williams. On these recordings the style was closer to the conventional city blues, even though his phrasing still had some of the looseness of the holler, and he often used the hummed interludes of the work songs.

Example 32

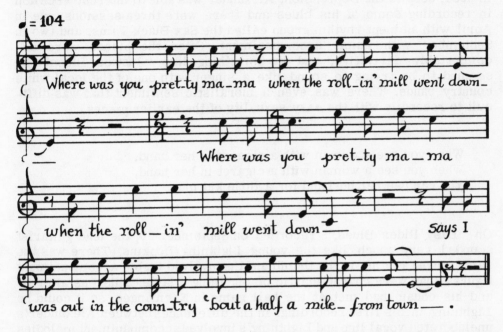

He generally stayed within the three line stanza form, and his texts were not distinctive, but he was often very open in his sexual imagery. The "Rolling Mill Blues" had the verse,

> When you gets to yoyoing you jumps it up and down.
> When you gets to yoyoing you jumps it up and down.
> But when you learn how to yoyo you turn it 'round and 'round.

and he elaborated on the image of the yoyo - a child's toy that moves up and down a string-in pieces like "Peaceful Blues."

> "I'm going to climb my woman's belly like a yoyo do a string."

The singing for the more conventional pieces was clear and direct, but in the pieces like "Awful Moaning Blues" there was considerable use of the melisma on the hummed tones. He seldom used the mordents that Lemon Jefferson had taken from the work song, but his holler style was more controlled than Lemon's irregular rhythms and vocal phrasing. For the country pieces he used a four or five note scale, often adding the flatted seventh for the more conventional pieces. Also unlike Lemon he was influenced by other singers, and a blues like "Double Crossing

201

Blues" recorded in June, 1929, - once past Little Hat Jones' usual hurried introduction - became almost a complete imitation of Lonnie Johnson's style, even to the opening phrases of Jones' guitar solo. Lonnie lived in Dallas for months at a time during this period, and Alexander had been with him in New York and in San Antonio for a number of sessions so the influence was probably a direct one.

In 1934, despite the Depression, Alexander was able to interest Vocalion in recording some of his blues and there were three sessions, one in April with an inept rhythm group called the Sax Black Tams, and two in September with guitar accompaniment. Often the pieces were uncomfortably derivative, and in something like "Justice Blues" he seemed to be trying to sound like a singer with one of the local white country bands. There was even a moralistic sentiment that was difficult to reconcile with the easy sexuality of the earlier pieces.

> When you see a woman with a cigaret in her hand,
> When you see a woman with a cigaret in her hand,
> You can use her husband for a little kid man.

On "Easy Rider Blues," recorded on September 30, the lead guitarist sounded very much like the young Lightning Hopkins. There was the same picked rhythm in the thumb and the involved treble accompaniment figures that were characteristic of Lightning's style. This was after he and his cousin had met at the ball game in Normangee, so it could be Lightning in his first recording. In the differences between Alexander's unelaborated vocal line and Lightning's involved accompaniment melodies there were already the seeds of the fullest development of the Texas style.

When the war was over Alexander was again singing around Texas. He was a burly, dark man, with some aggressiveness still left from his prison experience. Lightning said that he had been sent up for "...singing them bad songs - 'Some works undercover like a bull hogs eye' - and they sent him down." In 1946 or 1947 he was living in Houston, and Mrs. Ann McCullum made an audition. recording of his singing with Lightning accompanying him. The audition was for Alladin Records in Hollywood, and she had to travel to California with the artists that she chose. As Lightning remembers she asked "Do you want to make a thousand dollars?..." But she was uncomfortable around Alexander and took Amos Milburn with her instead. His last session seems to have been the Houston recording he did for Freedom Records in the spring of 1950, "Bottoms Blues" and "Crossroads," "Benton's Busy Bees," accompanied by Leon Benton on guitar and Edwin Pickins, piano. His style, by this time, had become almost indistinguishable from the dozens of other Texas singers who were recording at this period.

Alexander was perhaps too much involved with the commercial blues market to leave as distinctive a group of recordings as Lemon Jefferson, or the songster Henry Thomas, but the work song style, even when he first began recording in 1927, was no longer so closely tied to the blues. It was however, the seed from which so much had grown, and in his changing style there can be heard some of the changes in the blues themselves, as they moved from the dusty air of the country roads to the noise and the dim light of the roadhouses and the city night clubs.

15. SOME OTHER TEXAS SINGERS

Even in the relative sparseness of the blues recorded in Texas, the elements that were to become the mature Texas style were strongly marked. Columbia records did considerable recording in Texas in the late 'twenties, much of it with the great Texas religious singer Blind Willie Johnson, who was living in Waco. In Dallas the company worked with a number of blues men, among them Bobby Cadillac, Perry Dixon, Will or Bill Day, Billiken Johnson, Coley Jones, and Alex Moore, but the music was not strongly local in its styles. Cadillac and Dixon, who sang with piano or piano and guitar accompaniment, were influenced by the commercial city blues. Probably they were accompanied by the local musician Whistlin' Alex Moore, who also recorded for Columbia during this period. Coley Jones was advertised as "...the new Bert Williams," but he seemed to have learned most of his songs from the old minstrel stage or from white folk sources. He even did a version of the Child Ballad "Our Goodman," with the title "Drunkard's Special." He was probably also a member of the Dallas String Band, a country string band that Columbia recorded during this period. The band was rough and noisy, but they had considerable musicality and one of their compositions "Dallas Rag," has become popular as a folk instrumental piece.

In their singing the Dallas men represented the strong influences on Texas music, the country pieces, the city blues, and, to a lesser extent, the work song prison music. Johnny Head, a Texas singer who recorded for Paramount in late 1927 or early 1928, did a "Fare Thee Blues Part 1 and 2," but his style showed considerable white influence and there was even a kazoo-guitar Charleston section in the accompaniment. Willard Thomas, another young Dallas singer, was influenced by Lonnie Johnson's recordings on several of his Paramount releases, but his "No Baby Blues" showed a strong Lemon Jefferson influence. Even on songs like his "Hard To Rule Woman Blues," while the vocal influence was Lonnie Johnson, the accompaniment was in a more ex-

204

pressive knife style. His Mississippi blues, "Poor Boy Blues," also had a knife accompaniment. One of his most interesting pieces was a prison blues with some of the feeling of Texas Alexander's "Levee Camp Moan Blues," although it was more regular in its rhythmic structure and verse form. Thomas, who recorded under the name "Ramblin'" Thomas, played his own accompaniments and his style was rhythmically less related to the vocal chant than was Alexander's. Thomas's piece with the prison chant overtones was also a "moan," "Sawmill Moan," probably to cover Alexander's successful recording the summer before.

Hey - hey, hey, hey.
Heya - hey, hey, hey.
And I had 'em all night and got 'em all again today.

And I wish I had my same old good girl back.
I wish I had my same old good girl back.
'Cause that's the only one that I ever did like.

How can I love you? How can I love you?
How can I love you, you stay out both night and day?
How can I love you, you treat me most any way?

I'm going to sing this time and I ain't going to sing no more.
I'm going to sing this time and I ain't going to sing no more.
'Cause my girl have called me and I got to go.

If I don't go crazy I'm sure goin' to lose my mind.
If I don't go crazy I'm sure goin' to lose my mind.
'Cause I can't sleep for dreaming, still can't sleepwalk for cryin'.

The accompaniment was mixed, using strummed chords as well as finger-picked linear patterns, but for most of the verses he made considerable use of drumming single note repetitions in eighths on the lower strings. Melodically the piece moved from the freer hummed verse that opened it, to more conventional verse melodies for the last verses.

The elements of the developing Texas style were even more evident in the singing of younger men like Little Hat Jones - there was a young, nervous sound to his music - than it was in the older men like Lemon and Texas Alexander. Little Hat had some of Alexander's sound in his voice, and he was working as Alexander's accompanist when he began recording in the spring of 1929, but he was also moving toward a newer sound in both the voice and the guitar. Alexander recorded in San Antonio on Saturday, June 15, using Jones and a second guitarist as accompaniment. He did eight sides, including the fine "Awful Moaning Blues," and then Little Hat did two sides, "New Two Sixteen Blues" and "Two String Blues," released on OKeh 8712. Despite his obvious nervousness the pieces were distinctly marked with the Texas style. He used the same melody for both of them, singing in a high voice

with the same mordent that both Lemon and Henry Thomas had used in their blues. The accompaniment was the alternate back and forth strum, rather than finger picking, with a melodic cadence that was surprisingly reminiscent of the pattern that the Virginia singer Luke Jordan used.

There seems to have been some interest in him by the OKeh field unit, and he recorded again the next Friday afternoon, June 21, doing four titles, and on these he was more assured. For "Hurry Blues" he used a Lemon Jefferson melody, but he was a little more adventuresome on the guitar than he had been the week before, alternating the finger strum with a picked melody in the thumb or forefinger. The vocal melody was begun high - an octave and a half above tonic - and the singing was very clearly phrased. The verses were undistinguished, but they were suited to his style

> I'm going, sweet baby, don't you want to go.
> I'm going, sweet baby, don't you want to go.
> I'm going somewhere's I never been before.

There was some use of nearly every element of the new Texas guitar style. On "Rolled From Side To Side Blues" there was a little alternate thumb work, with a doubled strum on the top strings, and on "Little Hat Blues" there was a hurried introduction like the openings he had used on some of the pieces he'd done with Alexander the week before, the tempo slowing when he began to sing. There was a girl's voice encouraging him on the last of the four sides he did, "Corpus Blues" or "Corkscrew Blues," and he finally said, "I can't pick it - I'm just learning how," and went into a boogie woogie passage on the bass strings.

OKeh was back in San Antonio a year later and Little Hat was recorded again. In the year his style had become more assured and all four of the pieces were strongly effective. "Cross The Water Blues" used a melody similar to one of Lonnie Johnson's standard melodies, but there was a syncopated boogie line in the guitar and a rich erotic description.

> I want you to take me home with you, baby, and ease me down
> across your bed.
> I want you to take me home with you girl, and ease me down
> across your bed.
> I want you to talk baby talk to me and then suck my tongue
> cherry red.

"Cherry Street Blues" was one of his best recordings, and it set the boogie bass patterns against an unvarying chord in the top strings and a rapidly moving rhythm. Although Jones had no opportunity to develop fully as a singer his music already had many of the elements that were to emerge in the Texas style as the long years of the 'thirties drifted into the Depression.

Dallas, like most southern cities, had small blues clubs that opened and closed in the Negro districts through the 1930's. The pianist Alex Moore worked steadily in the clubs through these years, and one of the singers who often worked with him was Willie Reed, one of the most interesting of the young Texas singers who managed to get onto record. He just managed to get on record, despite a number of sessions between 1928 and 1935. Of the fourteen titles listed in Dixon and Godrich only four were released, "Dreaming Blues" and "Texas Blues" from a 1928 session for Columbia, and "Some Low Down Groundhog Blues" and "All Worn Out and Dry Blues" from two Vocalion sessions in September, 1935. By the later sessions he had begun to fall into some of the styles that were popular on other recordings, but the 1928 session was unique in the Texas blues. He used one of the Texas vocal melodies, and the guitar accompaniment had some of the nervous movement of the alternate strum style, but he was finger picking in an open tuning. The guitar tone was hard, but there was a strength and inventiveness in the accompaniment patterns. He sang in a richer voice than other young singers like San Antonio's Little Hat Jones, and there was even some inventiveness in his verses. In "Texas Blues" he began,

"I'm gong out in west Texas where you can hear the wild dogs moan..."

It was unfortunate that Reed was unable to record more extensively, since he may have represented a less well-known Texas style. It was also unfortunate that two other Texas singers, Sammy Hill and Marshall Owens, recorded as little as Reed. Hill, who did two sides for Victor in Dallas in 1929, was more conventional in style than either Reed or Owens, but he sang with a sensitive and musical style, the voice clear and open with a slight vibrato on the held tones. On "Needin' My Woman Blues" he used the hummed chorus that was characteristic of most of the Dallas singers, its melody closely related to the same melody that Gertrude Perkins, Texas Alexander, and Ramblin' Thomas used in at least one of their Texas-oriented blues. Marshall Owens did four songs for Paramount in December, 1931, and there were elements of Lemon Jefferson's vocal melodies in his "Texas Blues," although his voice was darker and heavier. It was so much lower than the usual Texas blues voice that Owens may have been a northern Louisiana singer, or a Mississippian who was familiar with some of the Texas recordings. His "Try Me One More Time" was more in the songster tradition of Henry Thomas, or of the southern Louisiana songster "Rabbit" Brown. For both pieces the rhythms were very regular within a bar line pattern with a closer relationship to the "entertainer" guitar style than to the local blues styles.

Alex Moore was one of the most distinctive of the Texas pianists to record, as much as anything else for the piercing whistle on some of the pieces, as a break from his own singing. Moore was born in Dallas on November 2 , 1899, and began playing the piano when he was in his late 'teens. Some of his early recording was as an accompanist, but he also did six titles as "Whistlin' Alex Moore" for Columbia in 1929, and four more titles for Decca early in 1937. He was recently located in Dallas and recorded again for a small California blues company, Arhoolie Records, which is owned by the field collector and blues enthusiast Chris Strachwitz. His style has absorbed a number of influences since his earliest years and there is a florid extravagance to the melodic material in the right hand as he tries to crowd in as much of the new concepts as he can. His voice is not strong, but there is an insistence in the left hand rhythms, and he uses a variety of bass styles, from the walking bass and the ragtime bass of the older period, to the open chords of well-known performers like Albert Ammons and Pete Johnson.

Although a number of Texas pianists were recorded there was no highly idiomatic local style like Skip James'. Generally the music was derivative. There has always been a tendency for some singers, especially men who do a lot of club entertaining, to pick up popular recordings and styles. Big Boy Knox, who recorded in San Antonio in March, 1937, had a great deal of this quality. He was another of the younger Texas pianists with some of the Leroy Garnett style, "Blue Man Blues" on Bluebird BB B-6952, was Bumble Bee Slim's "I Keep On Drinking," and "Eleven Light City Blues," on Bluebird B-6904, was derived from Kokomo Arnold's recordings, even to the use of Kokomo's distinctive compound verse melody. In "Texas Blues" Knox sang that he was born in Louisiana and moved to Texas, but there was nothing in his music that would relate him to Louisiana. Black Ivory King, whose real name was Dave Alexander, had a more individual piano style, and his "Flying Crow," named for a southern train, had some of the feeling of the piano "train" pieces that were popular with the boogie pianists of the 'twenties.

> Flying Crow leavin' Port Arthur, why they come to
>   Shreveport to change their clothes.
> Flying Crow leavin' Port Arthur, why they come to
>   Shreveport to change their clothes.
> They don't take water in Texarkana, and for Ashdown they'll
>   keep on through.

> Twenty-five minutes from (Evelyn) for a cup of coffee and a
>   slice of cake.
> Twenty-five minutes from (Evelyn) for a cup of coffee and a
>   slice of cake.
> Flying Crow is heading for Kansas City and, boy, she just won't
>   wait.

> Yonder she goes she's gone, with a red and green light
>   behind.
> She's gone, she's gone, with a red and green light behind.
> Well now the red means trouble and the green means a rambling
>   mind.

209

> Well, I hate to hear that old fireman when he tones the bell.
>   (piano solo)
> spoken: Oh ring 'em a long time.
>
> Uum, Umm, Umm.

Other pianists, like Leon Calhoun who recorded for Vocalion as "Son Becky," or Harold Holiday, who was "Black Boy Shine" on Vocalion, were less individual.

The blues form for many Texas singers in the 'thirties became almost a constricting influence, and the music tended to cling to conventional three line melodic forms. There was, however, a development of the knife guitar style that may have been influenced by the "steel guitar" playing in the white country and western bands. The two best-known Texas blues men to use the heavy-necked steel guitar were Oscar Woods, "The Lone Wolf," who recorded for Decca and Vocalion in 1936, 1937, and 1938, and a younger singer who learned from him, Babe Kyro Lemon Turner, who recorded for the American Recording Corporation and for Decca in 1936 and 1937 as "Black Ace." Turner was born in 1905 in Hughes Springs, Texas, a small town in Harrison County. He grew up about seven miles from the Louisiana state line, and only about thirty five miles from the northern Louisiana town of Shreveport. The Depression forced him to try working in Shreveport when he was in his twenties and he met Woods there, an older man who was making a living playing at house parties and dances. Turner had already begun playing the guitar, but he learned the steel guitar technique from Woods, holding the guitar across his lap and using a glass medicine bottle as a slide. For both Woods and Turner the blues had become a fixed musical form, and there was little variation from the three line verse and conventional melodic material. Turner's pseudonym came from his Decca recording of "Black Ace," and he used the opening verse, "I am the black ace, I'm the boss card in your hand..." as an introduction to a radio program that he did for several months on Fort Worth's station KFJZ.

Even with the extensive recording of the 'thirties, however, the Texas blues style still lacked definition and focus. It was not until after the second World War, when local record companies sprang up in Houston and Dallas, that all the elements of the disparate Texas music environment finally were brought together and the Texas blues grew into the rich musical form that had been visible in the singing of Lemon Jefferson, Texas Alexander, and Henry Thomas.

Notes

THE AFRICAN BACKGROUND

1. J. David Sapir, notes to The Music of the Diola-Fogny of the Casamance, Senegal, Folkways Record FE 4323 (New York, 1965)

2. John Wesley Work, Folk Song Of The American Negro, (Nashville, Tenn., 1915)

3. Howard Odum and Guy Johnson, Negro Workaday Songs, (Chapel Hill, North Carolina, 1926)

4. Luis Felipe Ramon Y Rivera, "Rhythmic And Melodic Elements In Negro Music Of Venezuela," Journal of the International Folk Music Council, XIV (1962), 56-60.

5. Hugh Tracey, "Towards An Assessment Of African Scales," African Music Society Journal, II (1958), 15-20

6. A. M. Jones, "African Music in Northern Rhodesia and some other Places," The Occasional Papers of the Rhodes-Livingstone Museum, IV (1949), 11

7. Le Vaillant, 1781, quoted in Percival Kirby, The Musical Instruments Of The Native Races Of South Africa, (London, 1934)

8. John Wesley Work, American Negro Songs, (New York, 1940)

CHAPTER 2 - CHARLEY PATTON

1. Booker White, interviewed by John Fahey and Ed Denson, Bukka White, Mississippi Blues, Volume 1, Takoma Records B1001, (Berkeley, California, 1964)

2. Bernard Klatzko, notes to The Immortal Charlie Patton, Origin Jazz Library record OJL-7, (New York, 1964)

3. J. D. Short, interviewed by Samuel Charters, Son House and J.D. Short, Folkways Record FA 2467, (New York, 1963)

4. Klatzko, op. cit.

5. Son House, interviewed by Julius Lester, Sing Out, XV, 3. (1965) 38-45

6. Ibid.

7. Ibid.

CHAPTER 3 - SON HOUSE

1. Son House, op. cit.

2. Ibid.

3. Ibid.

4. Ibid.

CHAPTER 5 - ROBERT JOHNSON

1. Henry Townsend, interviewed by Samuel Charters, unpublished recording, 1962.

2. Son House, op. cit.

3. Ibid.

CHAPTER 7 - MISSISSIPPI/THE COUNTRY SINGERS

1. Son House, interviewed by Dick Waterman, quoted by Al Wilson, "Son House, A Biography and Analysis of his music," Boston Broadside (1965)

2. Son House, Lester, op. cit.

3. Klatzko, op. cit.

CHAPTER 8 - CENTRAL MISSISSIPPI AND JACKSON INTO THE 'THIRTIES

1. Arthur Rosenbaum, notes to Shirley Griffith, Saturday Blues, Prestige Bluesville Record 1087, (Bergenfield, New Jersey, 1963)

CHAPTER 12 - BLIND LEMON JEFFERSON

1. Samuel Charters, The Country Blues, (New York, 1959), 57

2. Ibid., 60

3. Lightning Hopkins, interviewed by Samuel Charters, Lightnin' Hopkins, My Life In The Blues, Prestige Record 7370, (Bergenfield, N.J., 1965)

CHAPTER 14 - "TEXAS" ALEXANDER

1. Lightning Hopkins, op. cit.

Records Cited

The recordings that were discussed at some length in the text have been listed below with their original date of recording, original issue number, and place of recording. The data has generally been taken from the Dixon and Godrich discography "Blues And Gospel Records, 1902 to 1942." Many of the recordings are currently available on reissue lp's, and these re-releases have been listed after the original recording data. It is only in recent years that there has been a great deal of reissuing in the country blues field, but already the amount of material available is extensive and growing steadily. The most important group of albums has been produced by Bill Givens and Pete Whalen for their "OJL", Origin Jazz Library, and their albums include two Patton collections, two Mississippi collections, a Henry Thomas collection, and two very valuable anthologies of the purest country blues from Mississippi, Alabama, Texas, and the East Coast. A complete catalog is available through Origin Jazz Library, 39 Remsen Street, Brooklyn Heights, New York.

Another group of albums, produced in close cooperation with the Origin Jazz Library to avoid duplication of material, is on the RBF label, and it includes two "The Country Blues" anthologies, as well as albums by artists like Sleepy John Estes and Blind Willie Johnson. Both RBF recordings and the Folkways albums listed below can be obtained from Folkways, 165 W. 46th Street, New York, New York. Also active in the re-issue field is the Blues Classics Label, with material from newer country styles, as well as recordings from the East Coast and Texas. The albums are available from Box 5073, Berkeley, California.

CHAPTER 1 - MISSISSIPPI

1. "Berta," Angola Prison Work-songs - Recorded by Harry Oster, Louisiana Folklore Society A-5.

CHAPTER 2 - CHARLEY PATTON

1. "Tom Rushen Blues," Para 12855, Richmond, Ind., June 14, 1929, OJL 7.

2. "High Sheriff Blues," Voc 02680, New York, Jan. 30, 1934, OJL 1.

3. "High Water Everywhere (Part 1 and 2)," Para 12909, Grafton, Wis., Dec., 1929, OJL 7.

4. "Moon Going Down," Para 13014, Grafton, Wis., July, 1930, OJL 1.

5. "Mississippi Boll Weevil," Para 12805, Richmond, Ind., June 14, 1929, Folkways FP 251.

6. "Down The Dirt Road Blues (Over The Sea Blues)," Para 12854, Richmond, Ind., June 14, 1929, OJL 7.

CHAPTER 3 - SON HOUSE

1. "Preachin' The Blues (Part 1 and 2)," Para 13013, Grafton, Wis., July, 1930, OJL 5.

2. "My Black Mama (Part 1 and 2)," Para 13042, Grafton, Wis., July, 1930, OJL 2.

3. "Dry Spell Blues (Part 1 and 2)," Para 12990, Grafton, Wis., July, 1930, OJL 11.

4. "Depot Blues (I Ain't Gonna Cry No More)," LC, Robinsonville, Miss., 1942, AFS L-59, Folkways FA 2467.

5. "My Black Woman," LC, Robinsonville, Miss., 1942, Folkways FA 2467.

CHAPTER 4 - SKIP JAMES

1. "22-20 Blues," Para 13066, Grafton, Wis., Feb., 1931.

2. "Special Rider Blues," Para 13098, Grafton, Wis., Feb., 1931.

3. "If You Haven't Any Hay Get On Down The Road," Para 13066, Grafton, Wis., Feb., 1931, OJL t.

4. "Cypress Grove Blues," Para 13088, Grafton, Wis., Feb., 1931.

5. "Hard Time Killin' Floor Blues," Para 13065, Grafton, Wis., Feb., 1931, OJL 5.

6. "Devil Got My Woman," Para 13088, Grafton, Wis., OJL 2.

CHAPTER 5 - ROBERT JOHNSON
(Selections marked * available on Columbia CL 1654).

1. "32-20 Blues," Voc 03445, San Antonio, Tex., Nov. 26, 1936.*

2. "Preachin' Blues," Voc 04630, San Antonio, Tex.. Nov. 27, 1836.*

3. "Hell Hound On My Trail," Voc 04630, Dallas, Tex., June 20, 1937.*

4. "I Believe I'll Dust My Broom," Voc 03475, San Antonio, Tex., Nov. 23, 1936.

5. "Love In Vain," Voc 04630, Dallas, Tex., June 20, 1937.

6. "Me And The Devil Blues," Voc 04108, Dallas, Tex., June 20, 1937.*

7. "Walkin' Blues," Voc 03601, San Antonio, Tex., Nov. 27, 1936.*

CHAPTER 6 - BOOKER WHITE (Selections recorded in Chicago, March 7 and 8, 1940)

1. "When Can I Change My Clothes," Voc 05489.

2. "High Fever Blues," Voc 05489.

3. "Sleepy Man Blues," OK 05743.

4. "Black Train Blues," Voc 05588.

5. "Good Gin Blues," OK 05625. Blues Classics 6

6. "Aberdeen, Mississippi Blues," OK 05743.

(Additional selections from these sessions available on RBF 1, RBF 203, RBF 9.)

CHAPTER 7 - MISSISSIPPI/THE COUNTRY SINGERS

1. Willie Brown, "Future Blues," Para 13090, Grafton, Wis., July, 1930, OJL 5.

2. Garfield Akers, "Jumpin' And Shoutin' Blues," Voc 1481, Memphis, January, 1930, OJL 8.

3. William Harris, "Bull Frog Blues," Gen 6661, Richmond, Ind., Oct. 10, 1928, OJL 5.

4. Reubin Lacy, "Mississippi Jail House Groan," Para 12629, Chicago, March, 1928, OJL 8.

5. Kid Bailey, "Mississippi Bottom Blues," Br 7114, Memphis, Oct. 15, 1929, OJL 5.

6. Kid Bailey, "Rowdy Blues," Br 7114, Memphis, Oct. 15, 1929, OJL 5.

7. Sam Collins, "Signifying Blues," Ban 32395, New York, Oct. 8, 1931.

8. Sam Collins, "Slow Mama Slow," Ban 32311, New York, Oct. 8, 1931, OJL 10.

9. King Solomon Hill, "Down On My Bended Knee," Para 13116, Grafton, Wis., Jan., 1932, OJL 10.

10. King Solomon Hill, "Whoopee Blues," Para 13116, Grafton, Wis., Jan., 1932, OJL 10.

CHAPTER 8 - CENTRAL MISSISSIPPI AND JACKSON INTO THE 'THIRTIES

1. Ishman Bracey, "Saturday Blues," Vic 21349, Memphis, Feb. 4, 1928, OJL 8.

2. Tommy Johnson, "Big Road Blues," Vic 21279, Memphis, Feb. 3, 1928.

3. Charlie McCoy, "That Lonesome Train Took My Baby Away," OK 8863, Atlanta, Dec. 15, 1930.

4. Tommie Bradley, "Window Pane Blues," Vars 6054, Richmond, Ind., Jan. 16, 1932.

5. George Torey, "Married Woman Blues," ARC 7-08-57, Birmingham, April 2, 1937.

6. Tommy McClennan, "Whiskey Head Man," BB B-8760, Chicago, Dec. 12, 1940.

CHAPTER 9 - ALABAMA

1. Ed Bell, "Mean Conductor Blues," Para 12546, Chicago, Sept., 1927.

2. Barefoot Bill, "Squabblin' Blues," Col 14526-D, Atlanta, April 20, 1930.

3. Willie Doss, "My Black Mare," Blues At Newport 1964, Part 2, Vanguard VRS 9181.

4. Barefoot Bill, "My Crime Blues," Col 14510-D, Atlanta, Nov. 4, 1929.

5. Ed Bell, "Frisco Whistle Blues," Para 12546, Chicago, Sept., 1927.

CHAPTER 10 - ALABAMA INTO THE 'THIRTIES

1. Jaybird Coleman, "Mean Trouble Blues," Gen 6245, Birmingham, Aug. 3, 1927, OJL 8.

2. George "Bullet" Williams, "Touch Me Light Mama," Para 12680, Chicago, May, 1928, OJL 2.

3. Wiley Barner, "My Gal Treats Me Mean (But I Can't Leave Her Alone)," Gen 6261, Birmingham, Aug. 15, 1927.

CHAPTER 11 - TEXAS

1. Ramblin' Thomas, "Poor Boy Blues," Para 12722, Chicago, Nov., 1928.

2. Henry Thomas, "Red River Blues," Voc 1137, Chicago, Oct., 1927, OJL 3.

CHAPTER 12 - BLIND LEMON JEFFERSON

1. "See That My Grave Is Kept Clean," Para 12585, Chicago, Oct., 1927, Folkways FP 253.

2. "Black Horse Blues," Para 12367, Chicago, May, 1926.

3. "Elder Green's In Town," OK unissued, Chicago, March 14, 1927.

4. "English Stop Time," OK unissued, Chicago, March 14, 1927.

5. "Blind Lemon's Penitentiary Blues," Para 12666, Chicago, Feb., 1928.

6. "Prison Cell Blues," Para 12622, Chicago, Feb., 1928.

7. "Bakershop Blues," Para 12852, Richmond, Ind., Sept. 24, 1929.

8. "Mean Jumper Blues," Para 12631, Chicago, Feb., 1928.

9. "That Black Snake Moan," Para 12407, Chicago, Oct., 1926.

10. "That Black Snake Moan No. 2," Para 12756, Chicago, March, 1929

11. "Bad Luck Blues," Para 12443, Chicago, Oct., 1926.

12. "Stocking Feet Blues," Para 12407, Chicago, Oct., 1926.

13. "That Crawlin' Baby Blues," Para 12880, Richmond, Ind., Sept. 24, 1929.

14. Walter Taylor and John Byrd, "Wasn't It Sad About Lemon," Para 12945, Grafton, Wis., April, 1930.

CHAPTER 13   HENRY THOMAS

1. "Run Molly Run," Voc 1141, Chicago, Oct. 7, 1927, OJL 3.

2. "Old Country Stomp," Voc 1230, Chicago, June, 1928, OJL 3.

3. "Texas Easy Street Blues," Voc 1197, Chicago, June, 1928, OJL 3.

CHAPTER 14   TEXAS ALEXANDER

1. "Levee Camp Moan Blues," OK 8498, New York, Aug. 12, 1927, RBF 9.

2. "Section Gang Blues," OK 8498, New York, Aug. 12, 1927, RBF 9.

3. "Rolling Mill Blues," OK 8751, San Antonio, Tex., Nov. 27, 1929.

4. "Justice Blues," Voc 02856, Fort Worth, Tex., Sept. 29, 1934.

CHAPTER 15 - SOME OTHER TEXAS SINGERS

1. Ramblin' Thomas, "Sawmill Moan," Para 12616, Chicago, Feb., 1928.

2. Little Hat Jones, "Hurry Blues," OK 8735, San Antonio, Tex., June 21, 1929.

3. Little Hat Jones, "Cross The Water Blues," OK 8829, San Antonio, Tex., June 14, 1930.

4. Black Ivory King, "Flying Crow," Decca 7307, Chicago, Feb. 15, 1937, Blues Classics 5.

Index

THE BLUESMEN.

DATE DUE

MAR 20 1995	
APR 20 1995	
APR 16 2000	
MAY 06 2005	

GAYLORD   PRINTED IN U.S.A.